RECORDED VERSIONS GUITAR

AUTHENTIC TRANSCRIPTIONS
WITH NOTES AND TABLATURE

John 5

Songs for Sanity

2 Damaged
12 Soul Of A Robot
24 Geinwith Envy
32 Sin
41 Behind The Nut Love
44 Blues Balls
53 Fiddler's
62 Gods And Monsters
71 2 Die 4
74 Death Valley
81 Perineum
96 Denouement
102 Guitar Notation Legend

Music transcriptions by David Stocker

ISBN 1-4234-0478-5

HAL•LEONARD® CORPORATION

7777 W. BLUEMOUND RD. P.O. BOX 13819 MILWAUKEE, WI 53213

Visit Hal Leonard Online at
www.halleonard.com

Damaged

Music by John 5

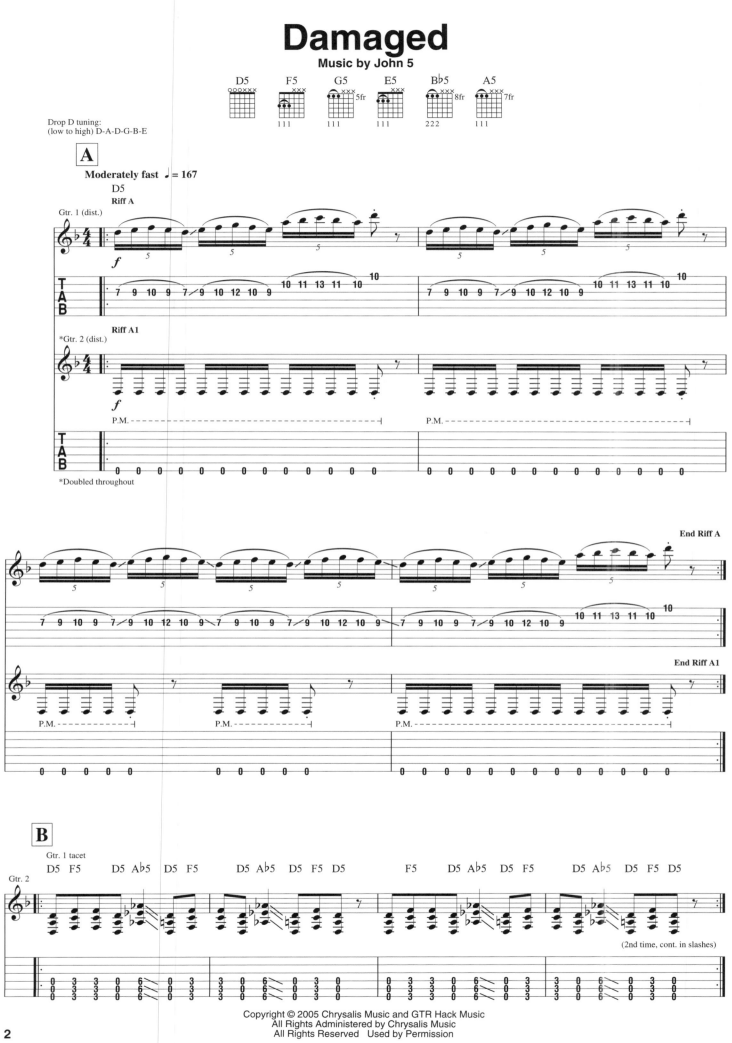

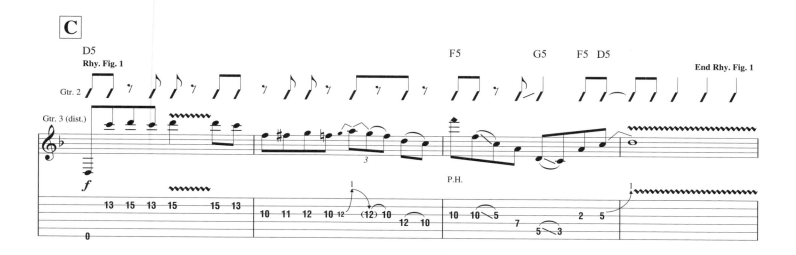

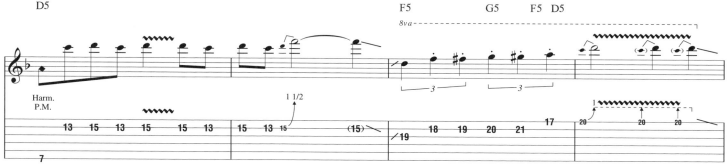

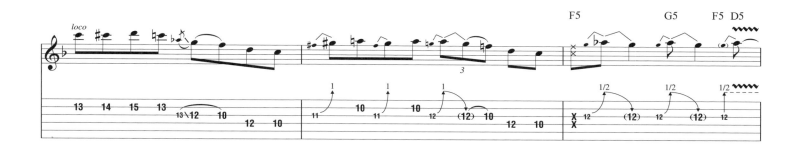

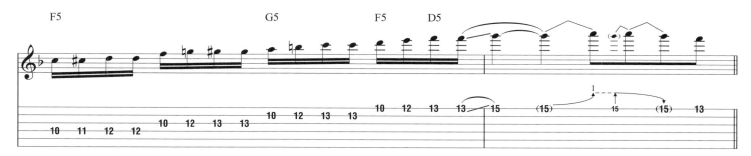

3

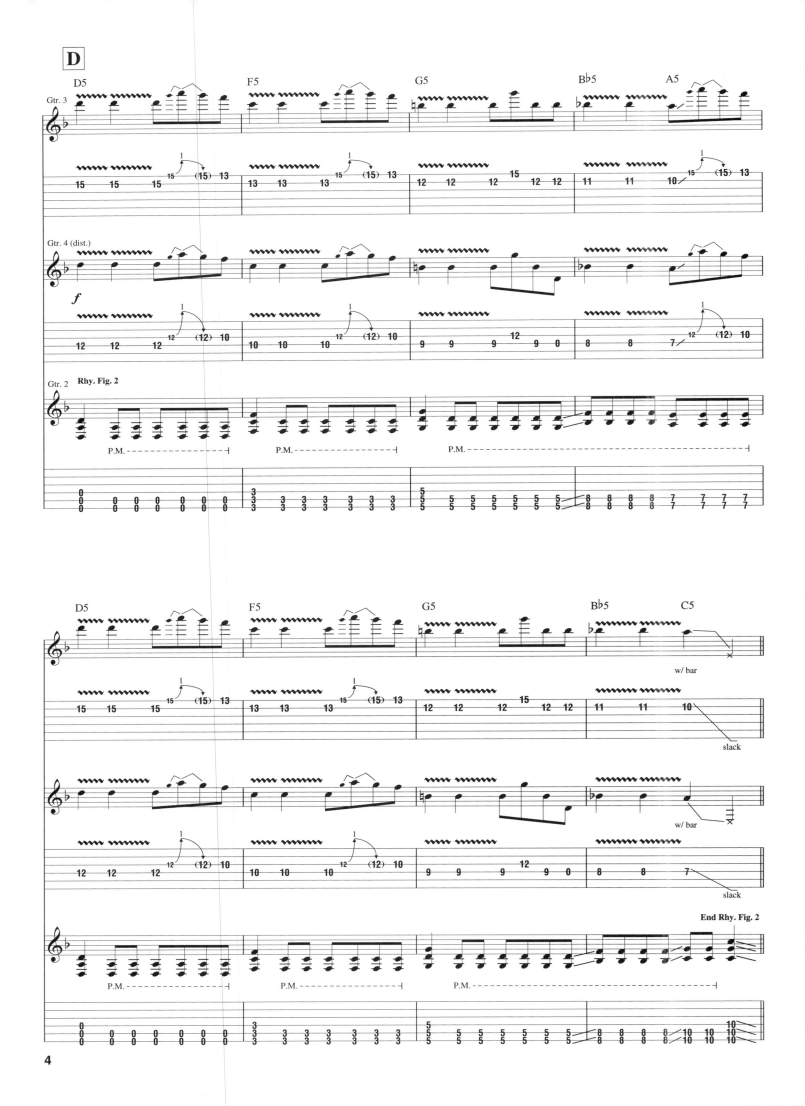

E

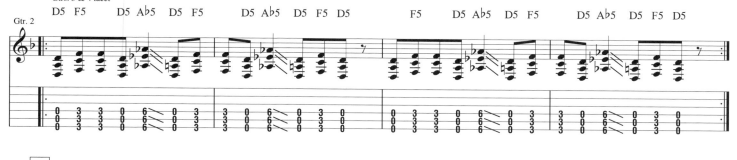

F

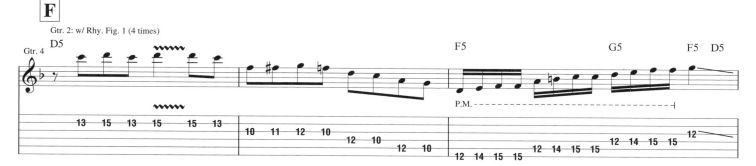

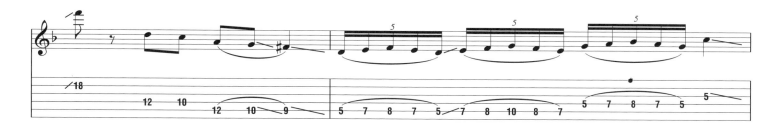

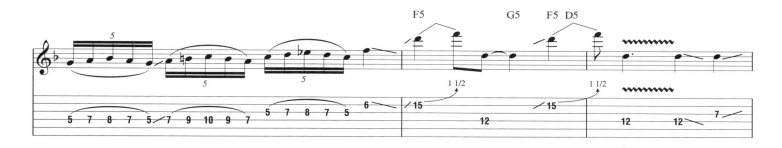

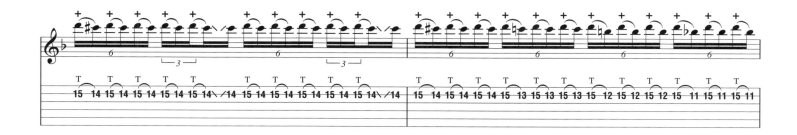

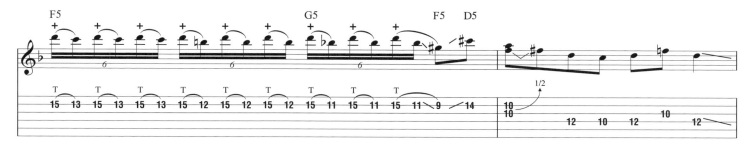

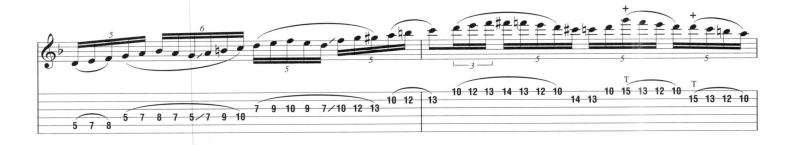

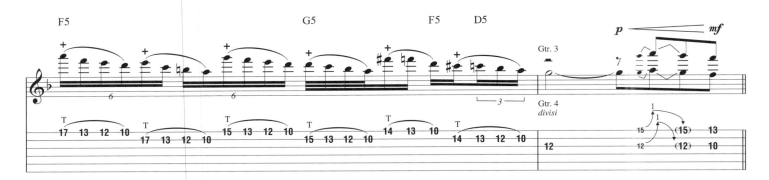

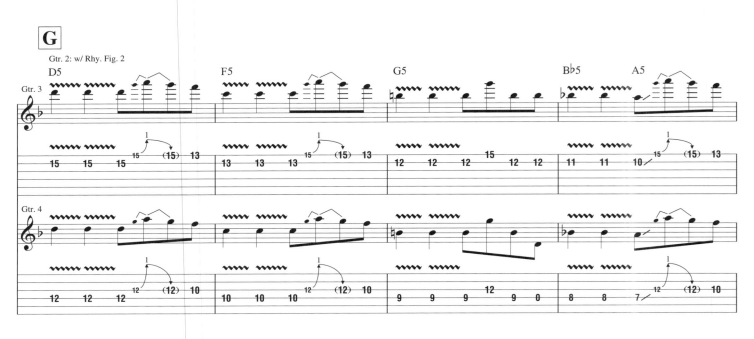

G

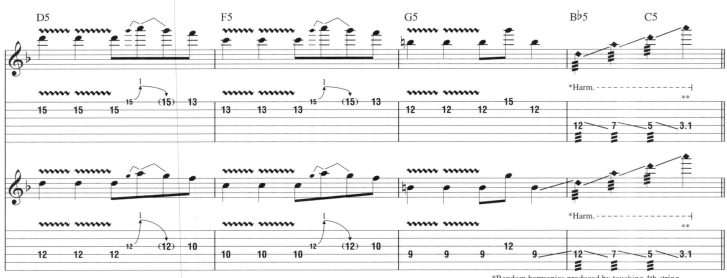

*Random harmonics produced by touching 4th string
and sliding in direction indicated on tab staff.
**Harmonic located one-tenth the distance between 3rd & 4th frets.

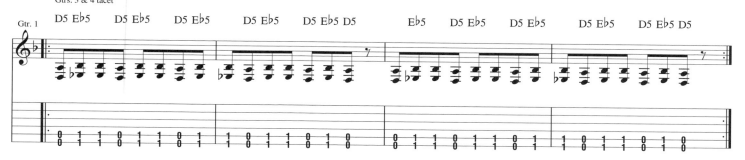

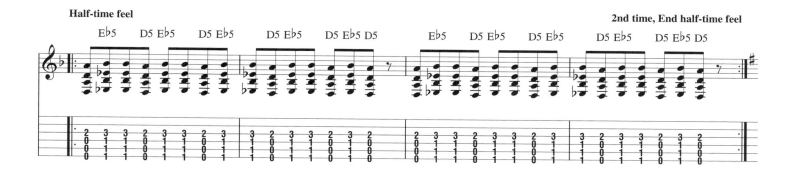

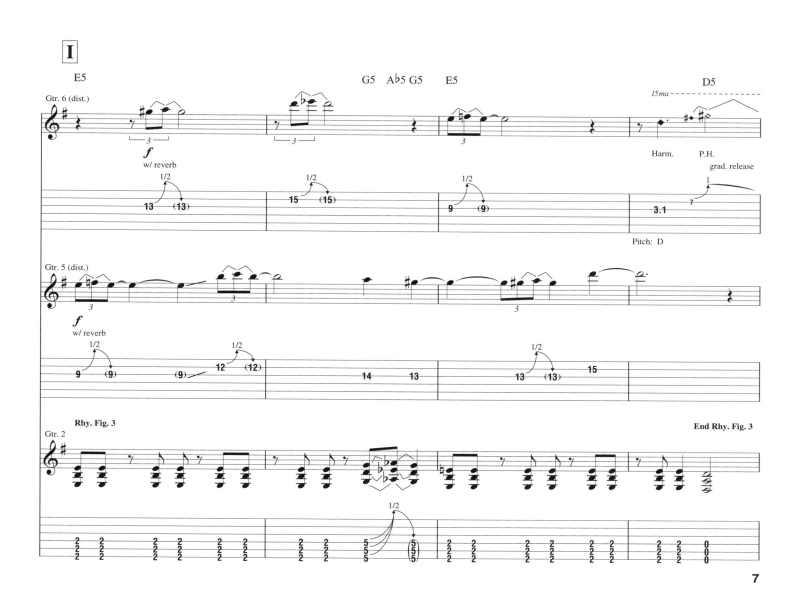

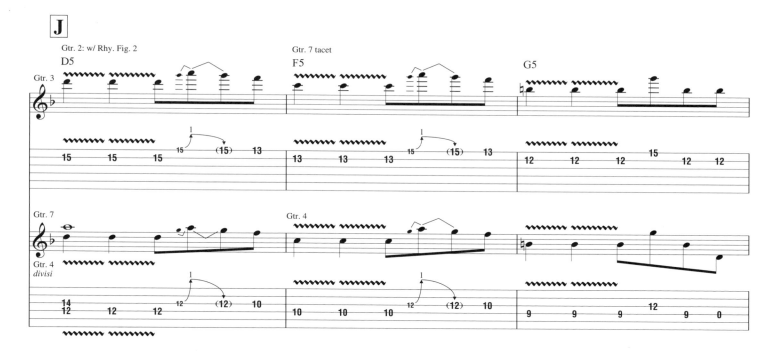

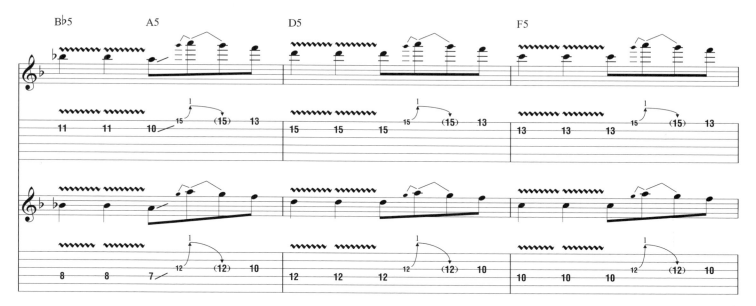

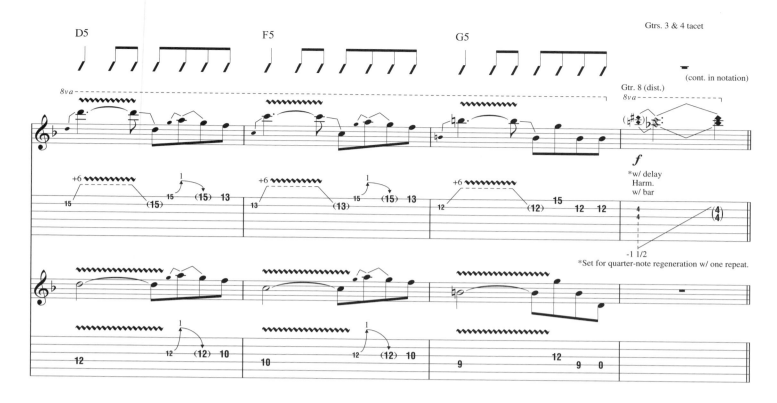

Gtrs. 3 & 4 tacet

(cont. in notation)

Gtr. 8 (dist.)

*w/ delay
Harm.
w/ bar

*Set for quarter-note regeneration w/ one repeat.

K

Gtr. 1: w/ Riff A (2 times)
Gtr. 8 tacet

D5

Gtr. 2

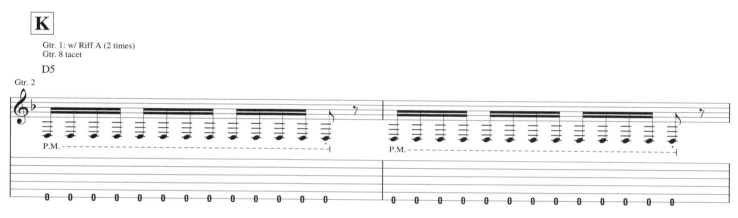

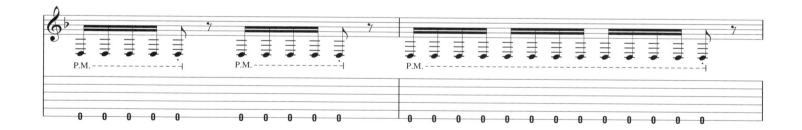

Gtr. 2: w/ Riff A1

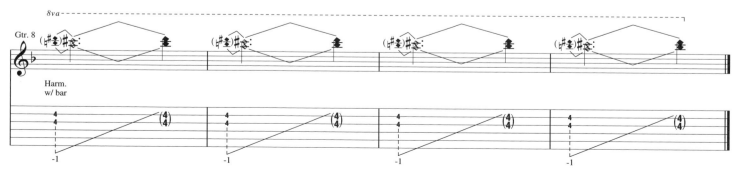

Gtr. 8

Harm.
w/ bar

Soul of a Robot

Music by John 5

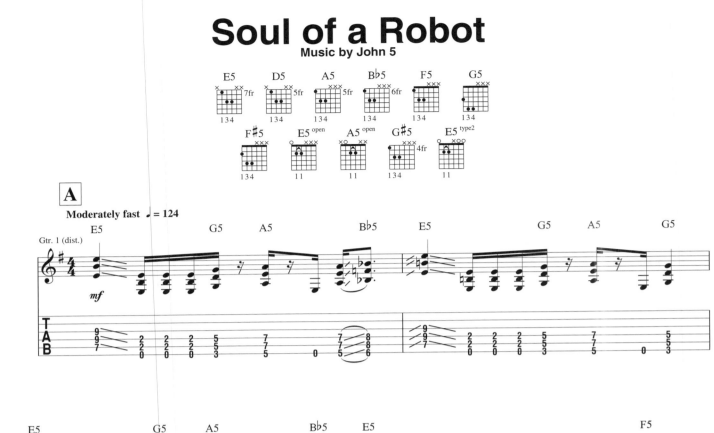

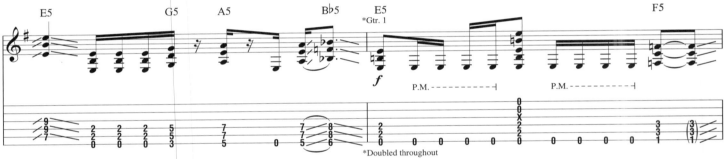

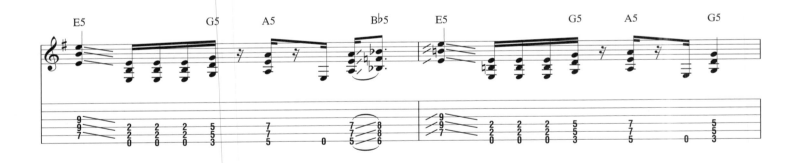

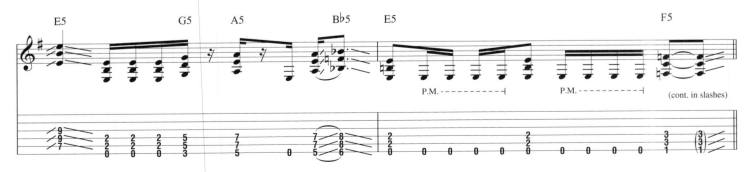

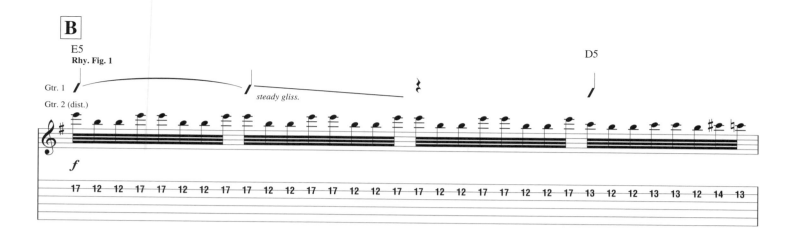

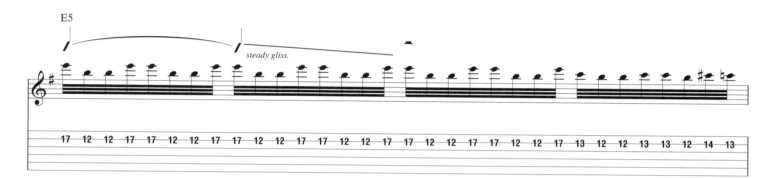

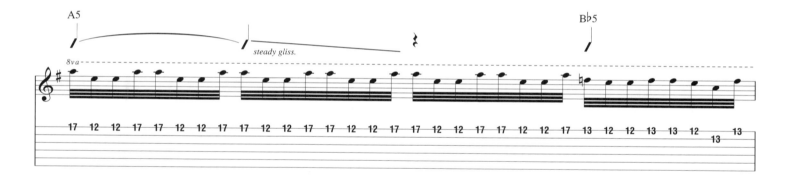

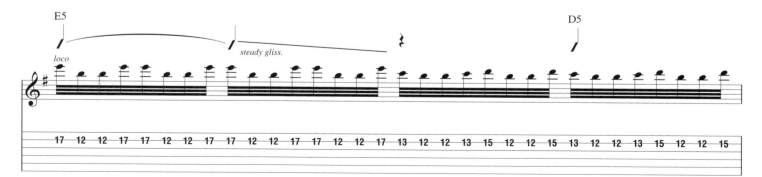

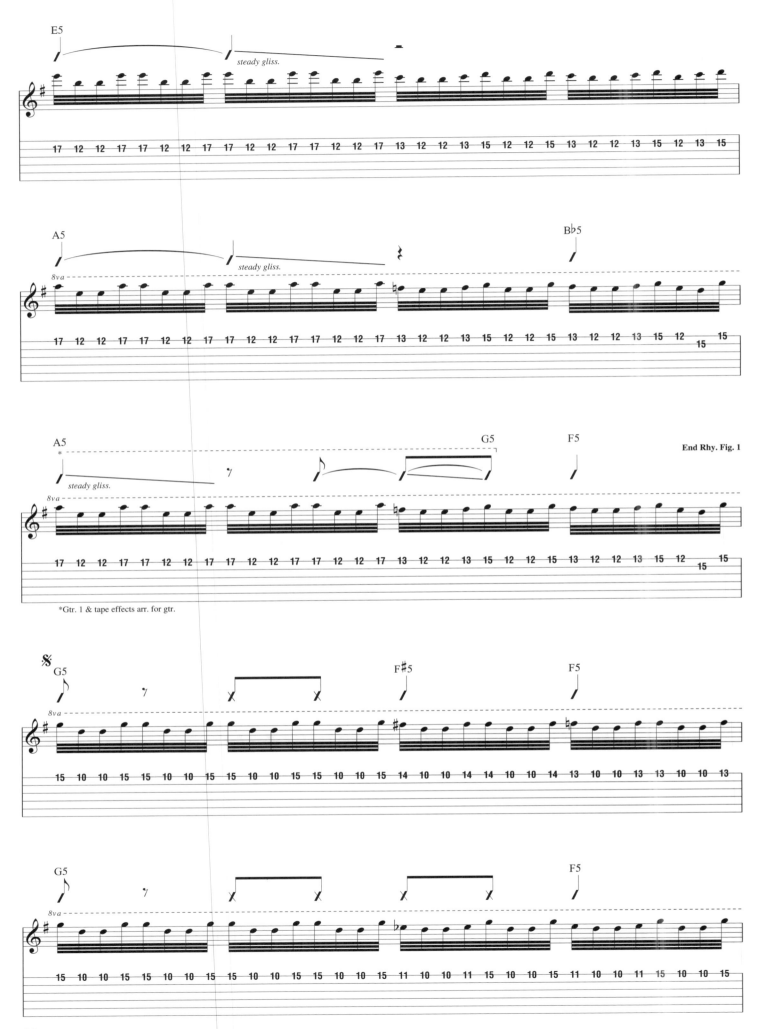

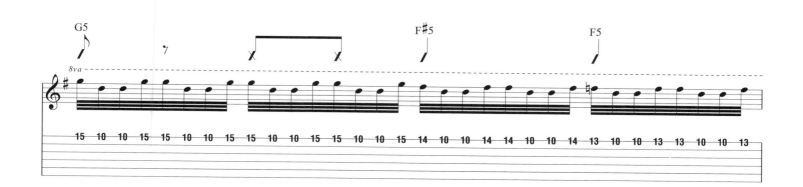

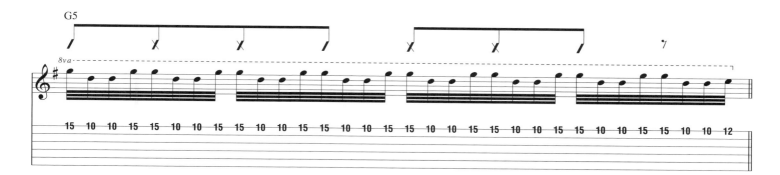

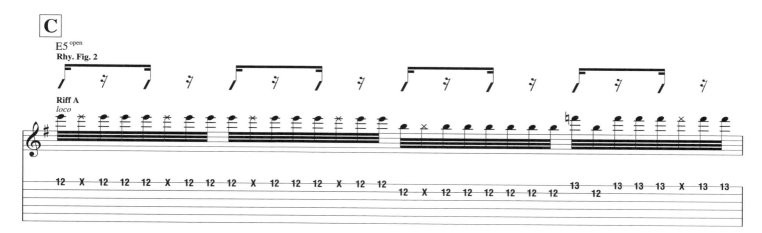

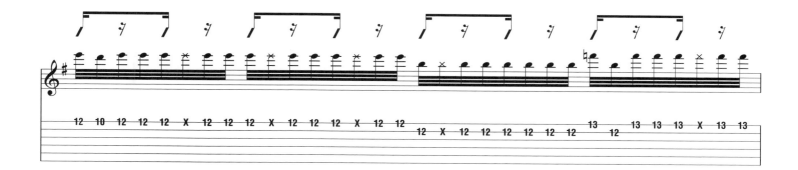

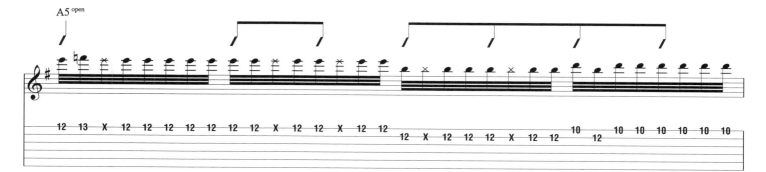

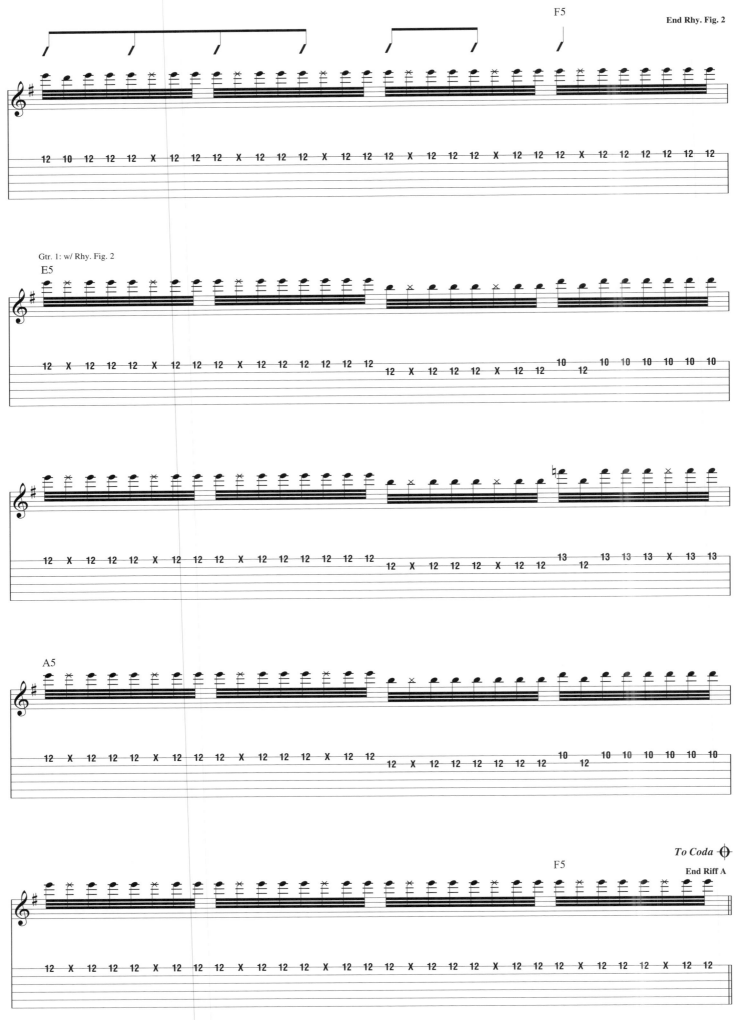

16

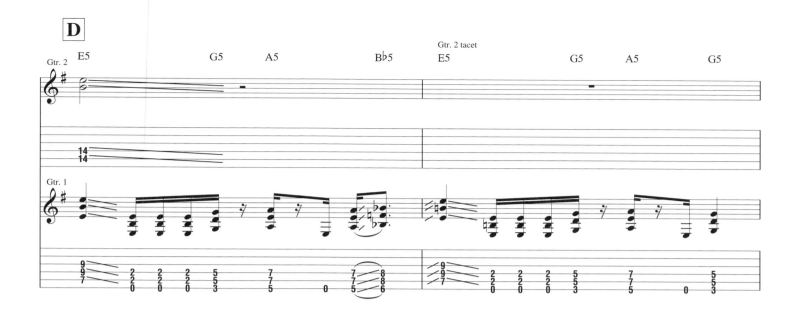

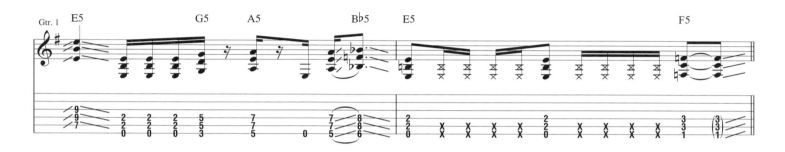

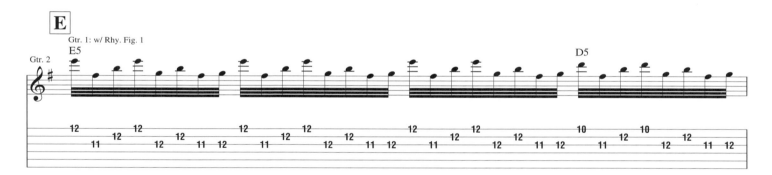

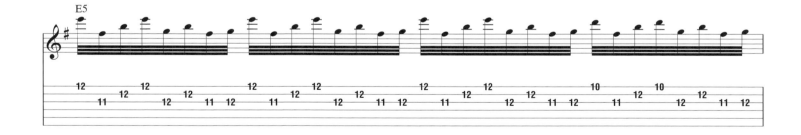

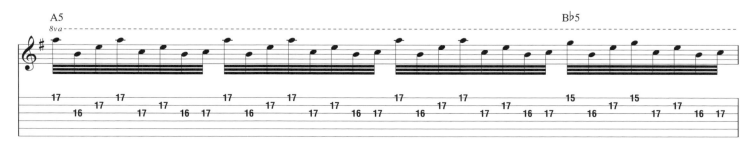

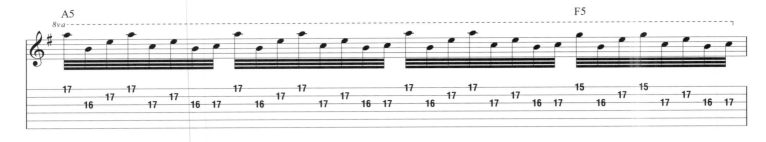

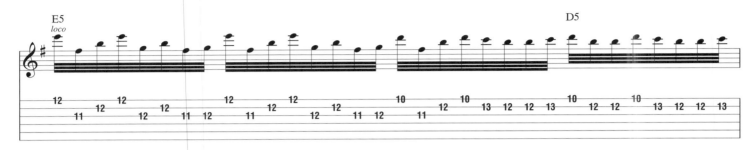

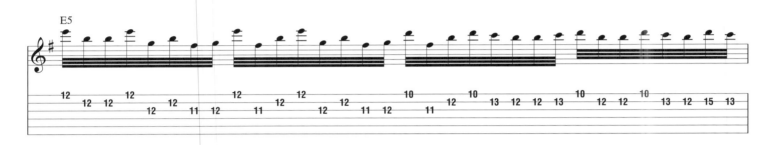

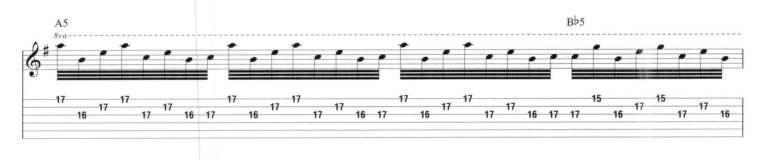

D.S. al Coda

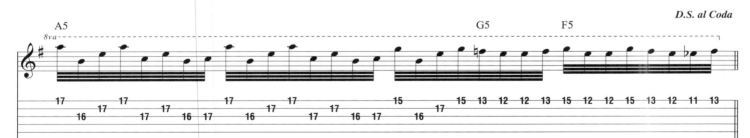

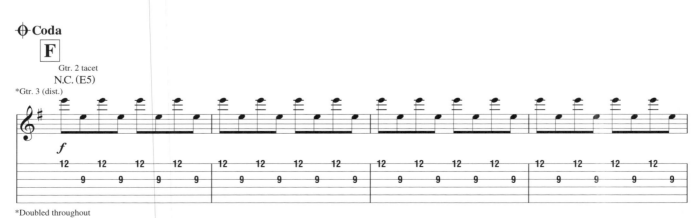

*Doubled throughout

*Chord symbols reflect overall harmony.

***Set for one octave below.

Gtr. 3: w/ Riff B

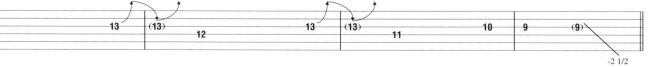

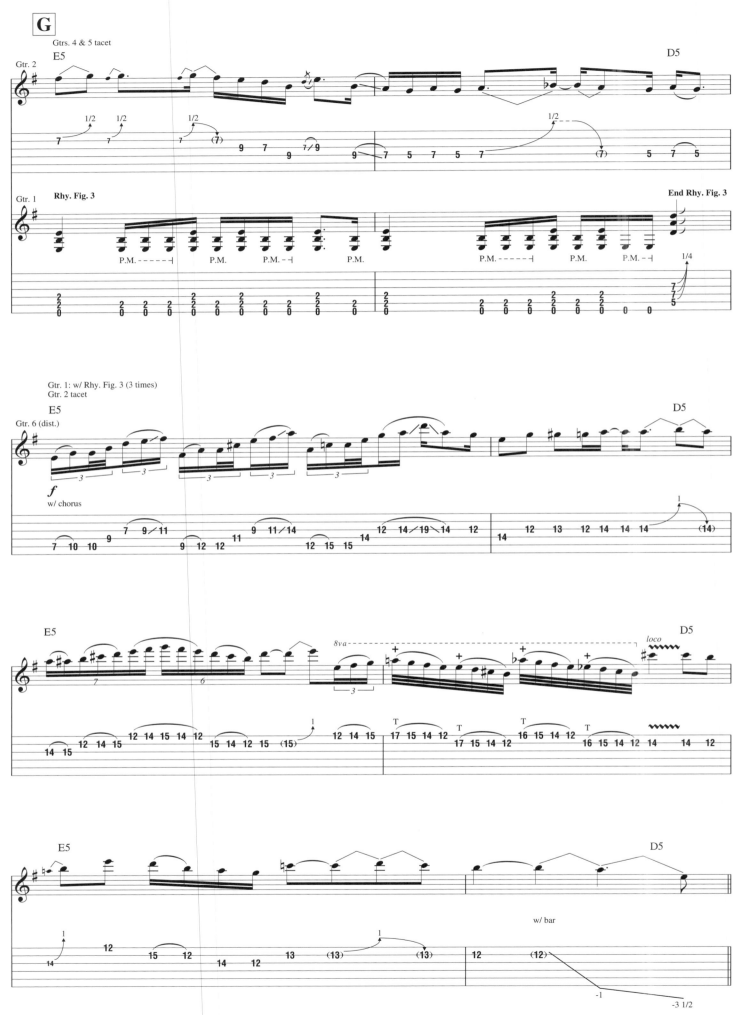

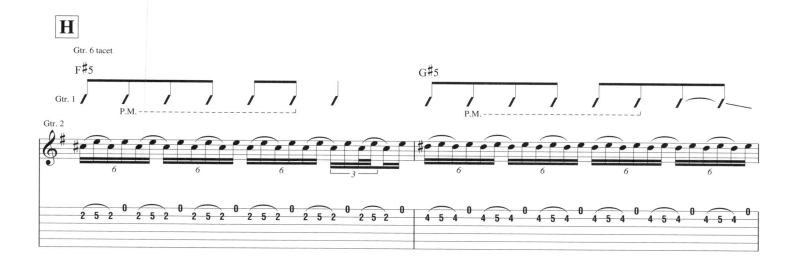

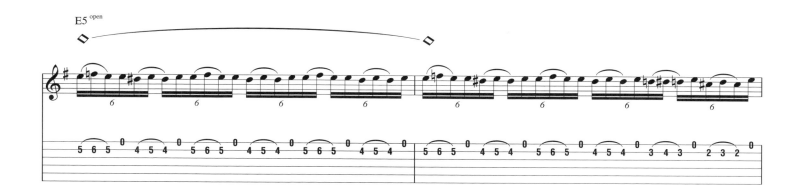

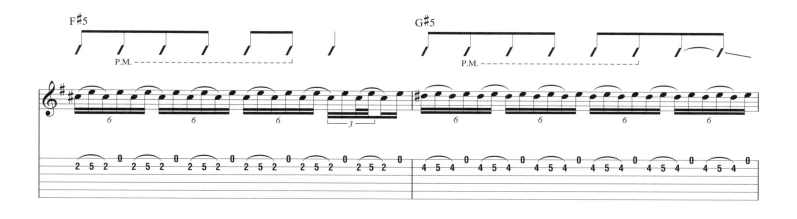

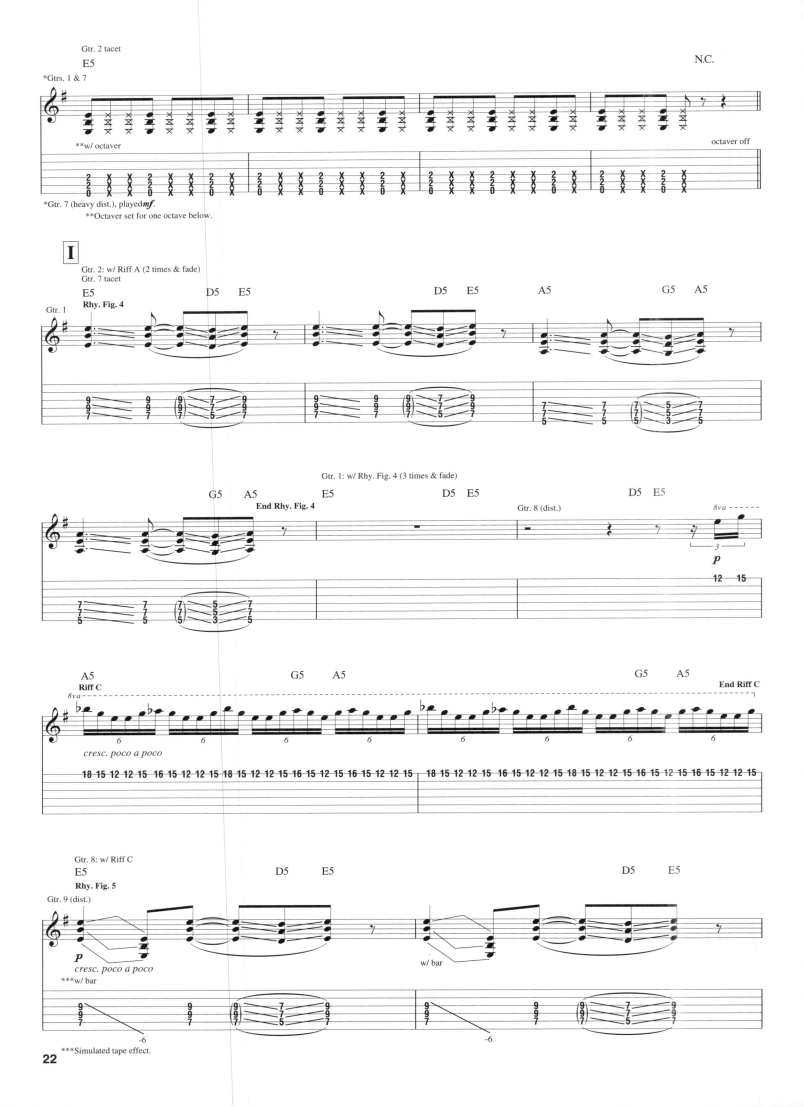

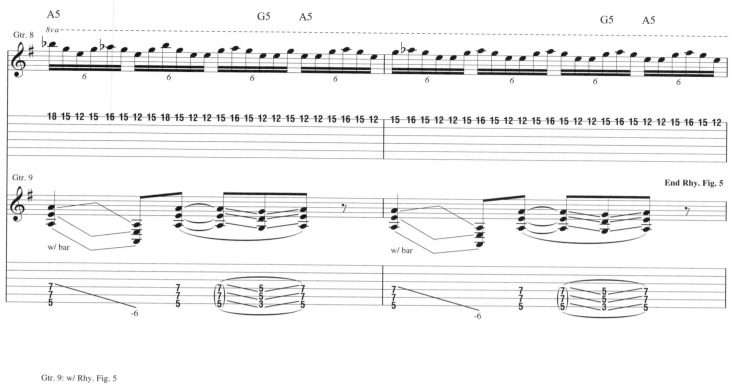

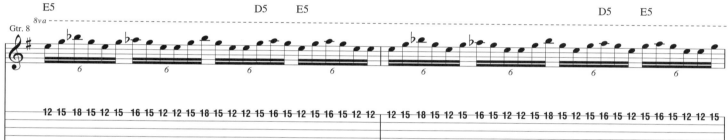

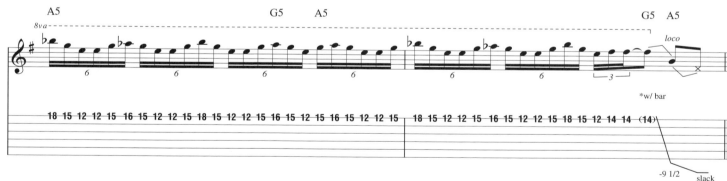

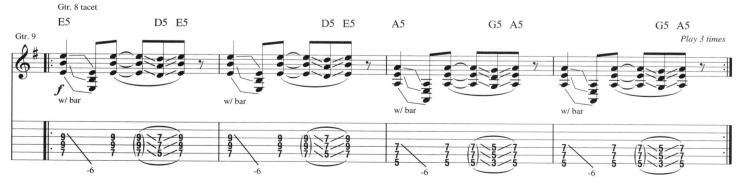

Gein With Envy

Music by John 5

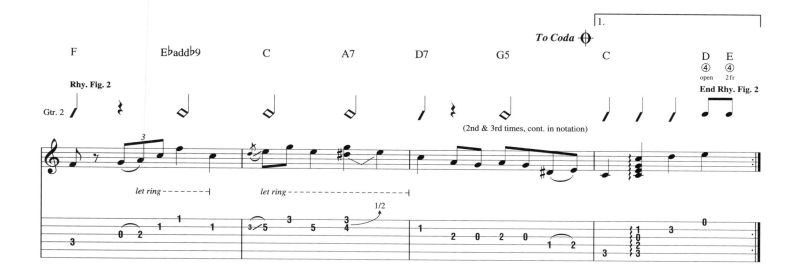

*Chord symbols reflect implied harmony.

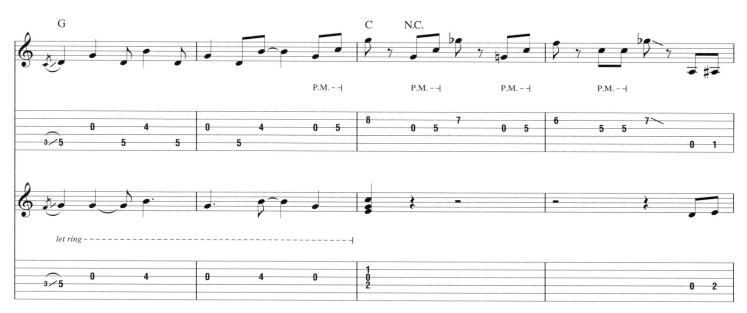

26

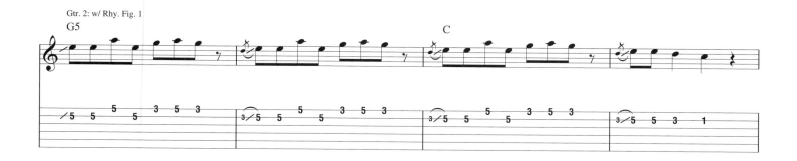

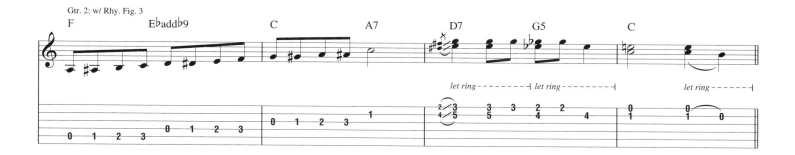

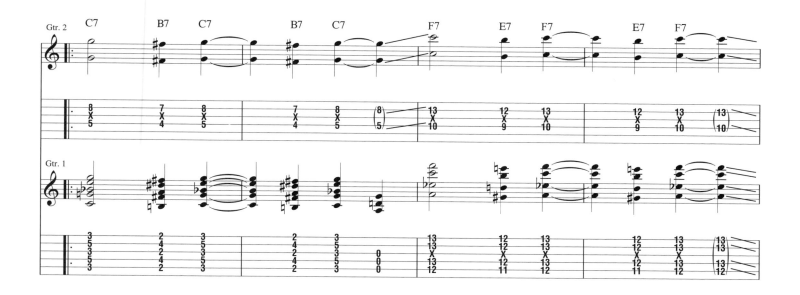

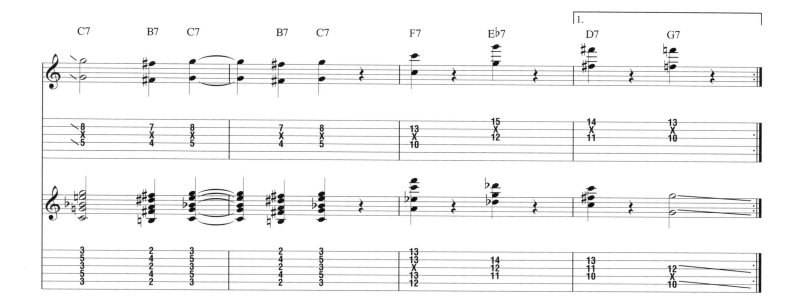

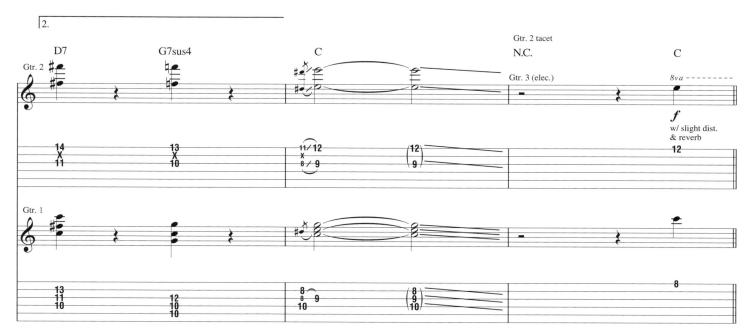

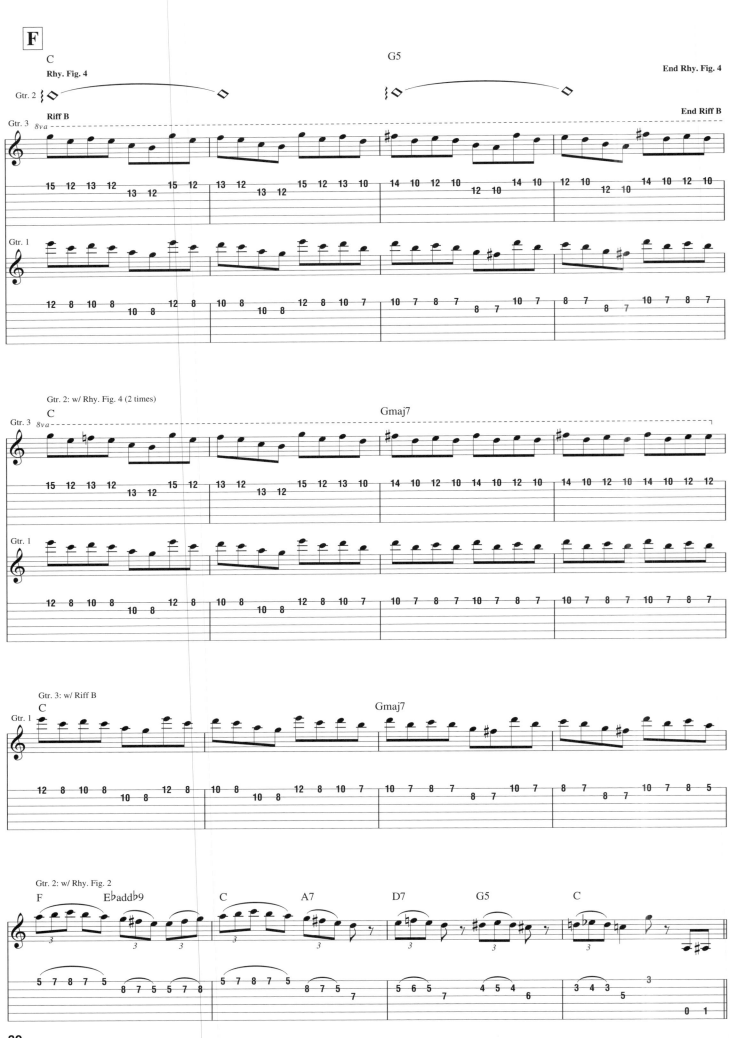

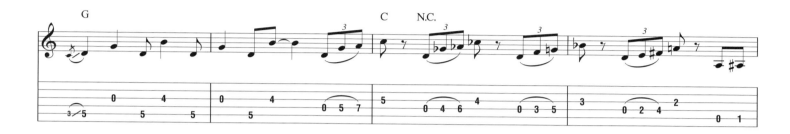

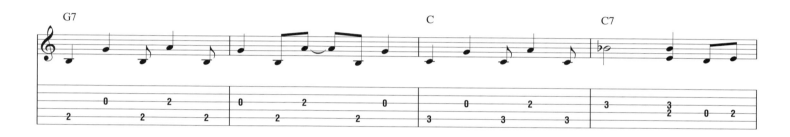

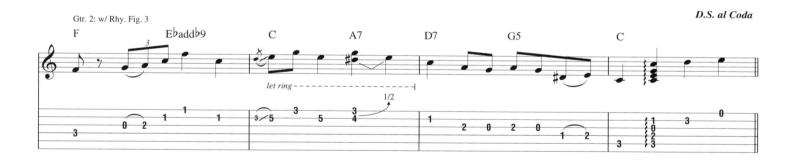

Sin

Music by John 5

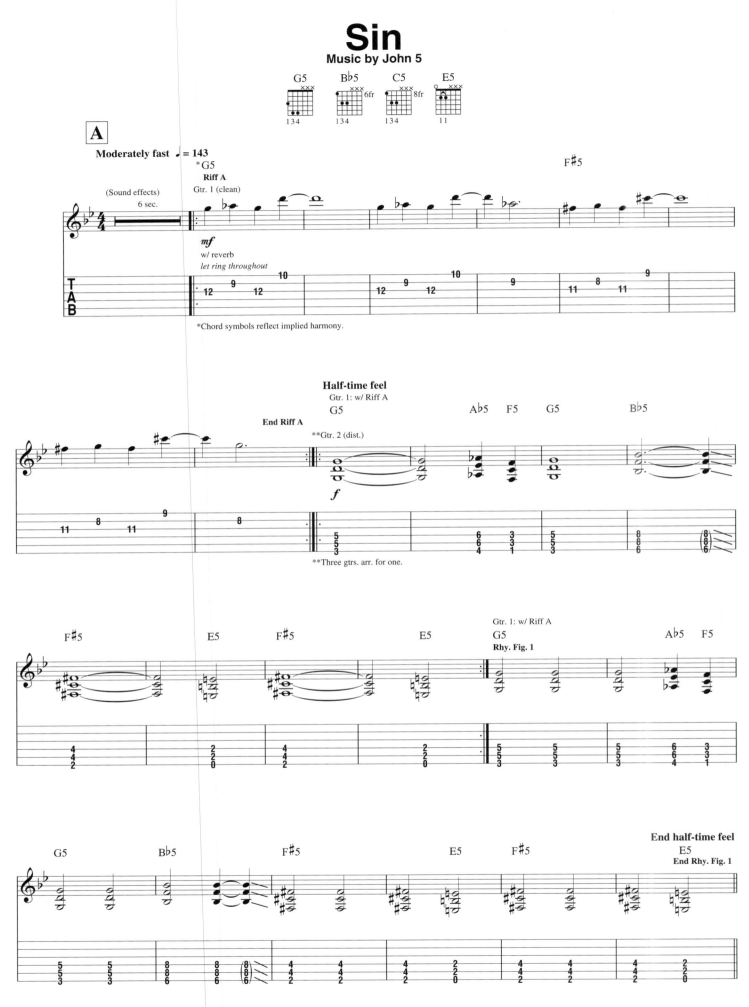

*Chord symbols reflect implied harmony.

**Three gtrs. arr. for one.

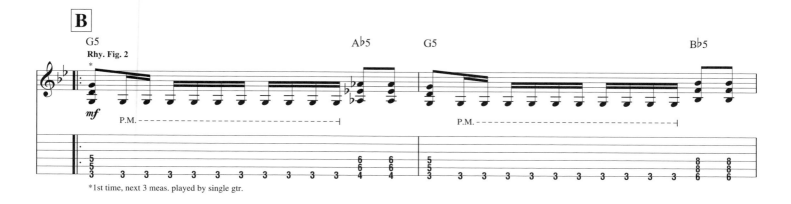

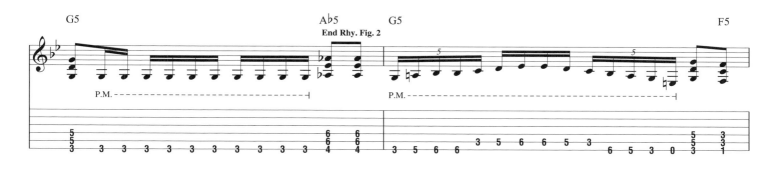

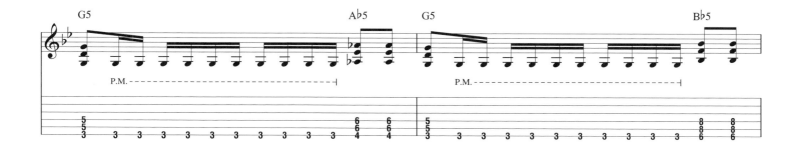

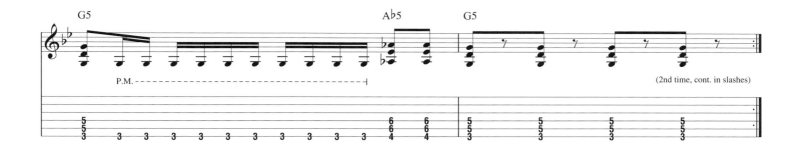

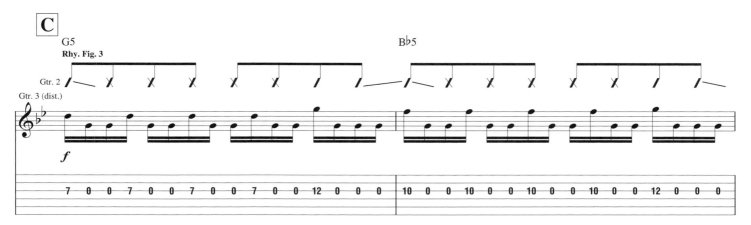

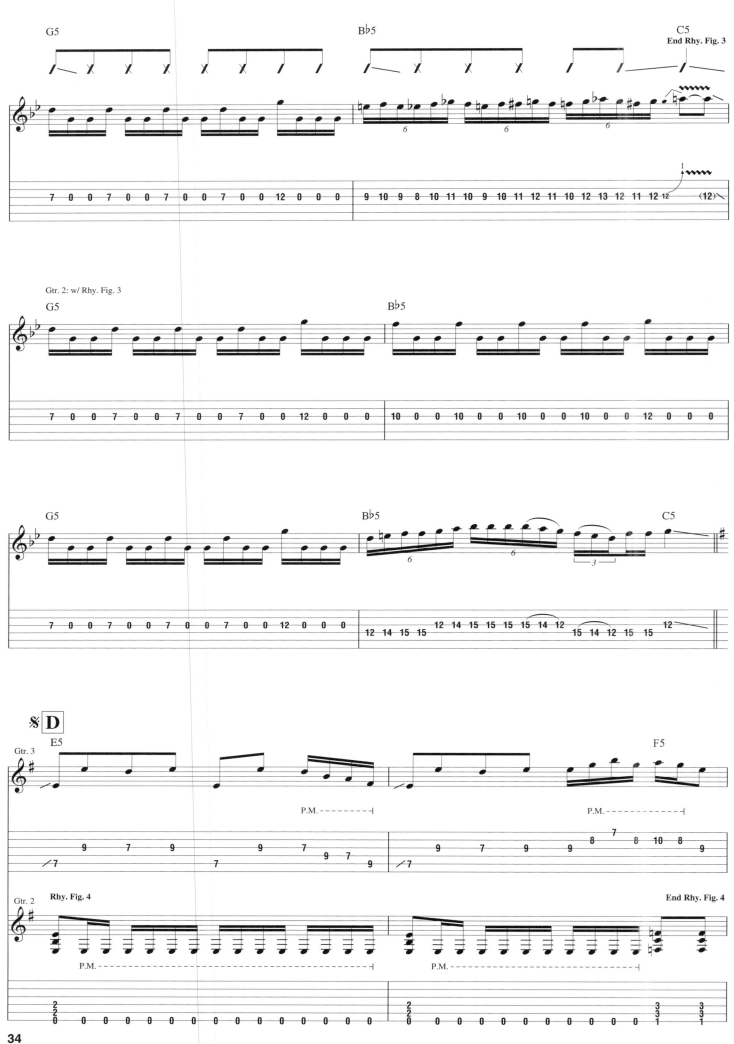

34

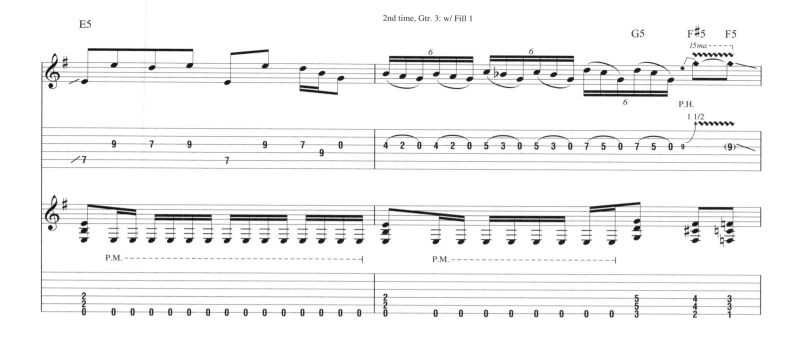

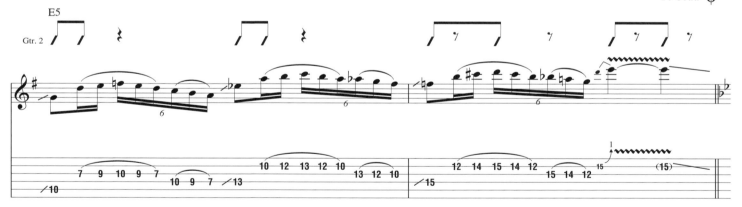

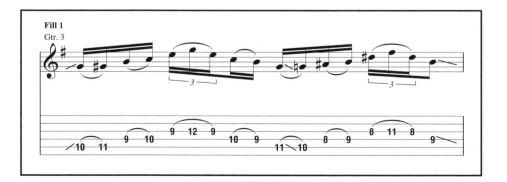

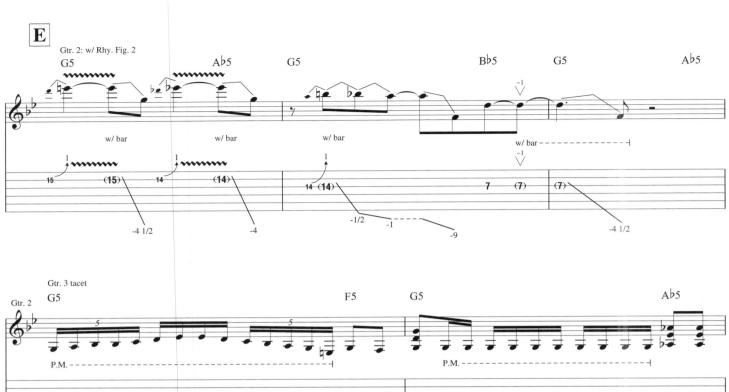

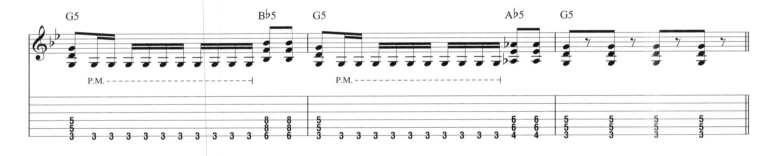

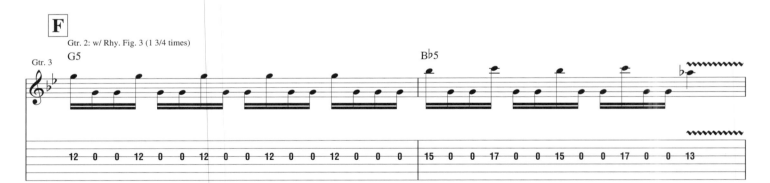

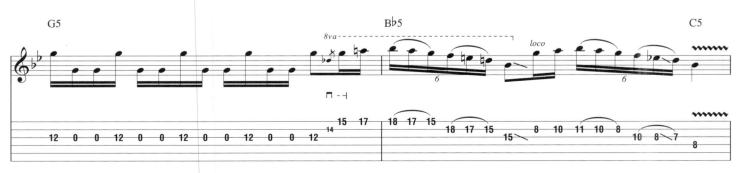

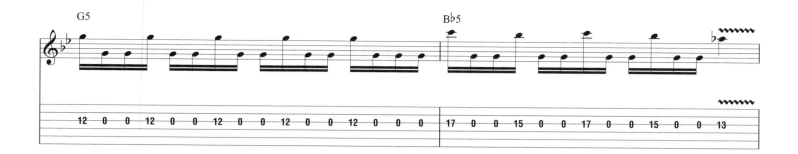

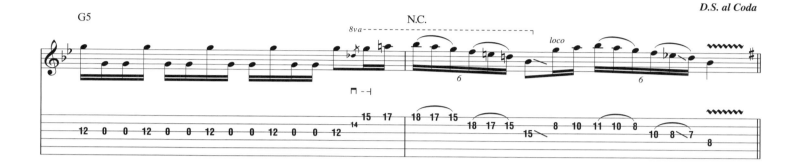

D.S. al Coda

Coda

$\boxed{\text{G}}$

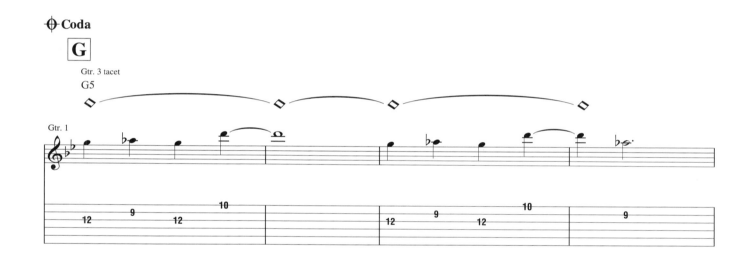

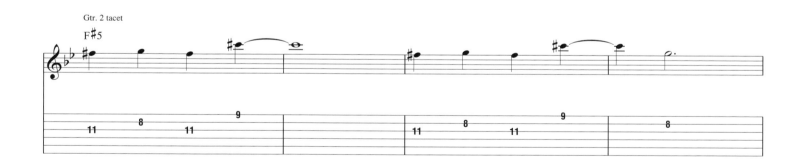

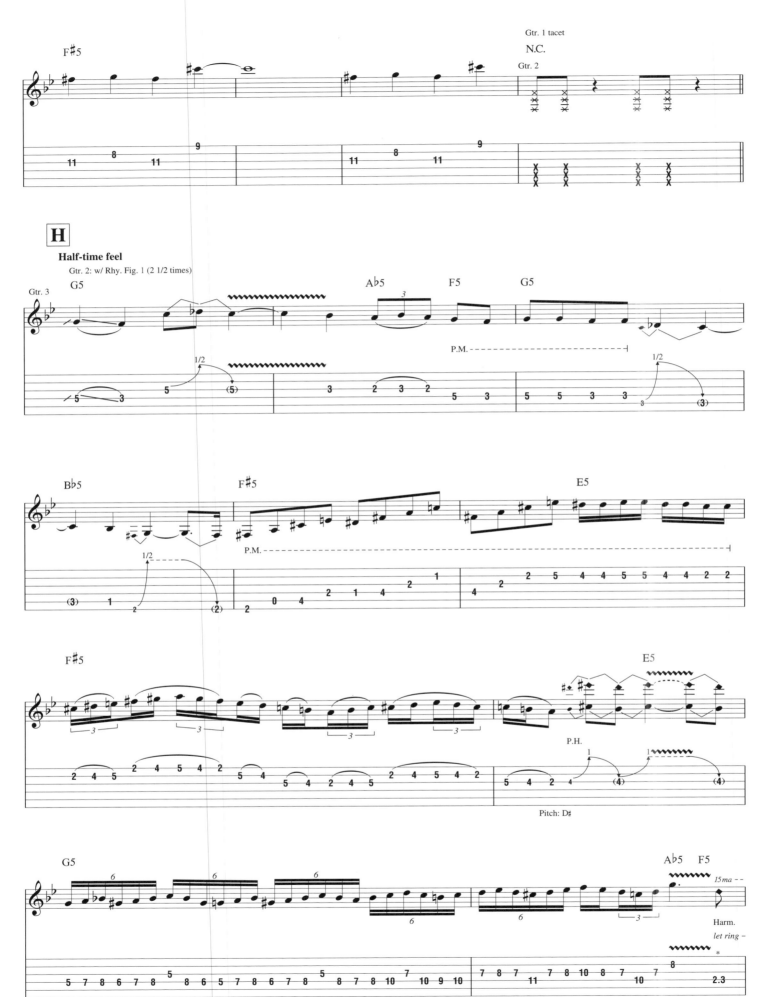

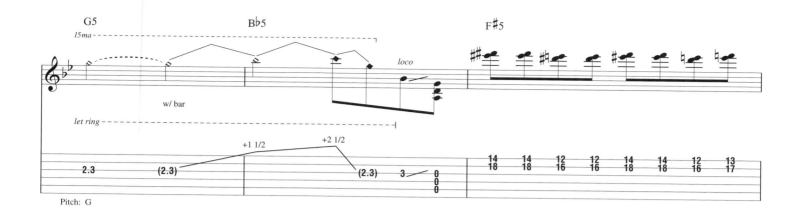

Pitch: G

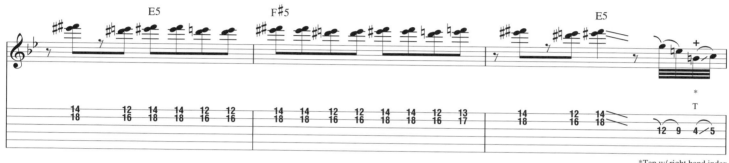

*Tap w/ right hand index
finger behind left hand,
next 4 meas.

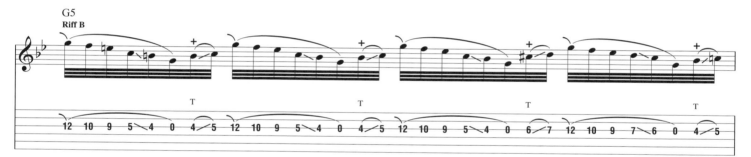

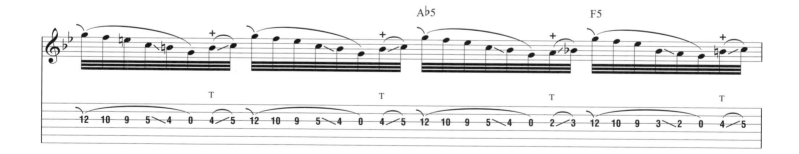

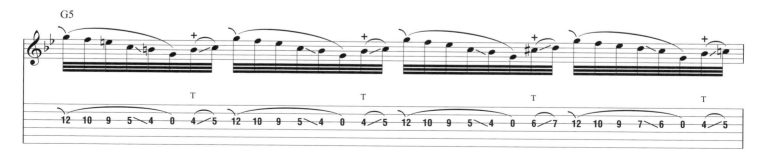

Behind the Nut Love

Music by John 5

Open D tuning:
(low to high) D-A-D-F♯-A-D

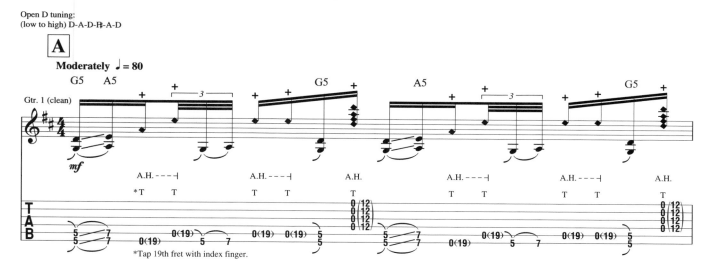

*Tap 19th fret with index finger.

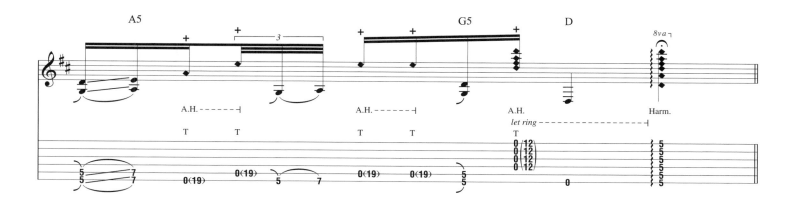

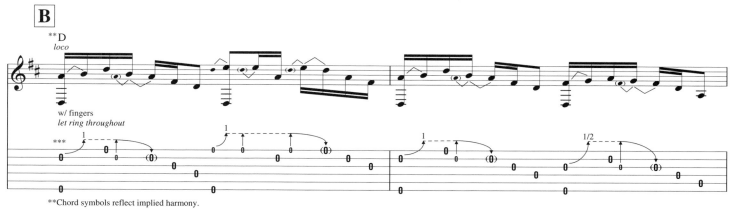

**Chord symbols reflect implied harmony.
***Bend strings behind the nut (next 7 meas.).

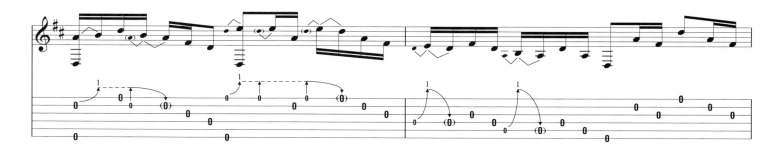

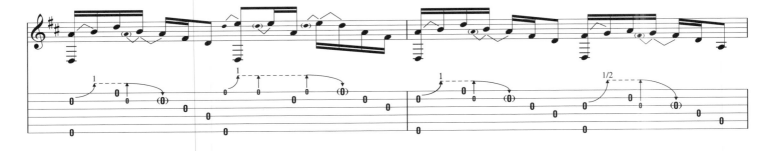

C

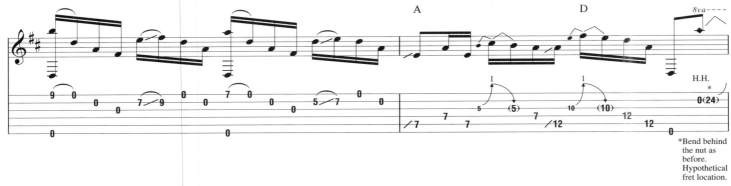

*Bend behind
the nut as
before.
Hypothetical
fret location.

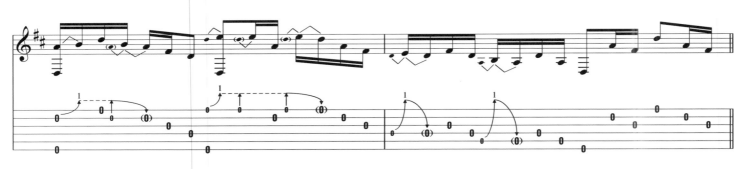

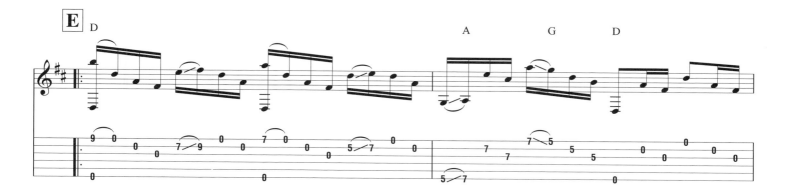

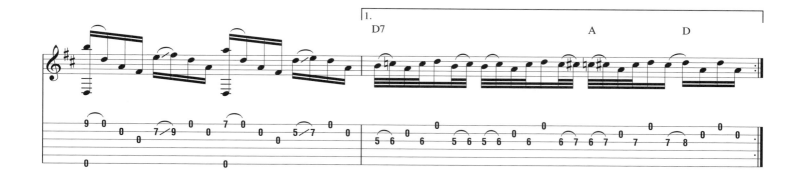

Pitch: D F# A D

Blues Balls

Music by John 5 and Kevin Savigar

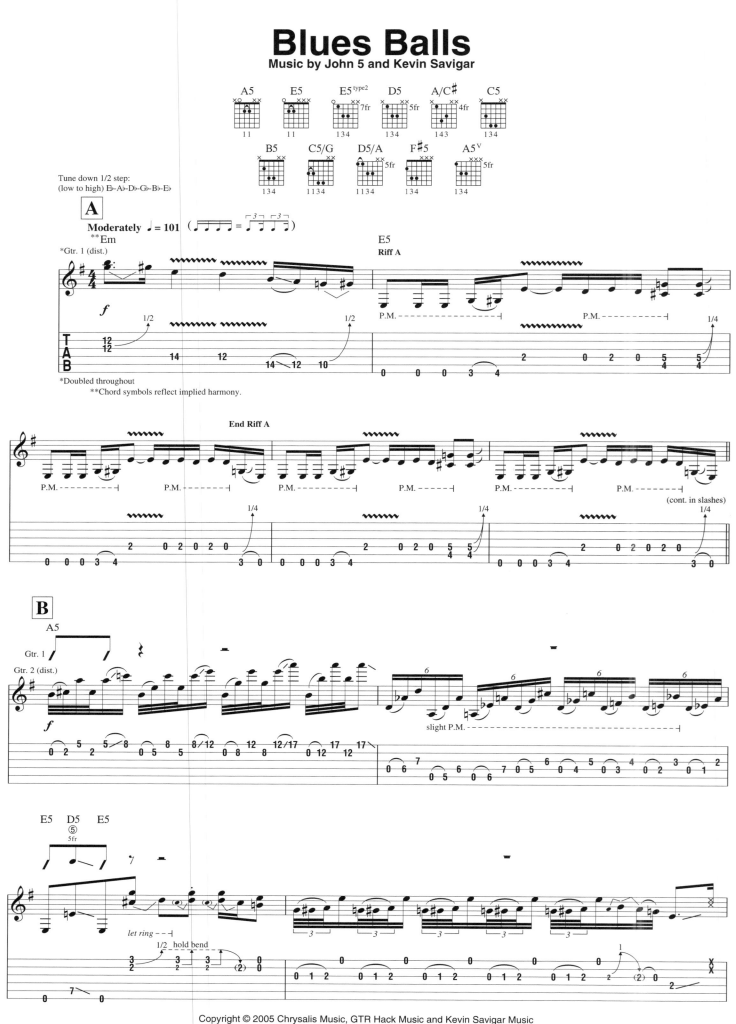

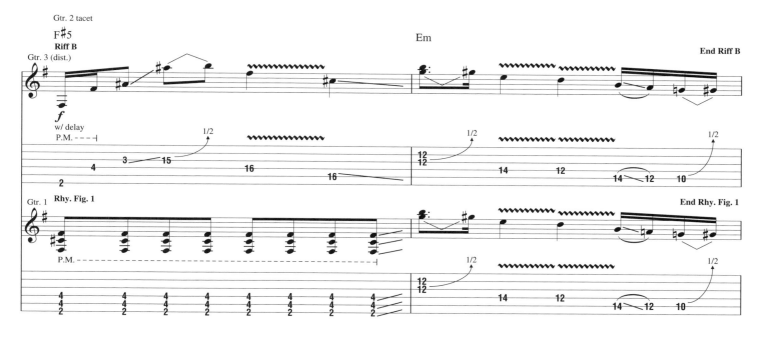

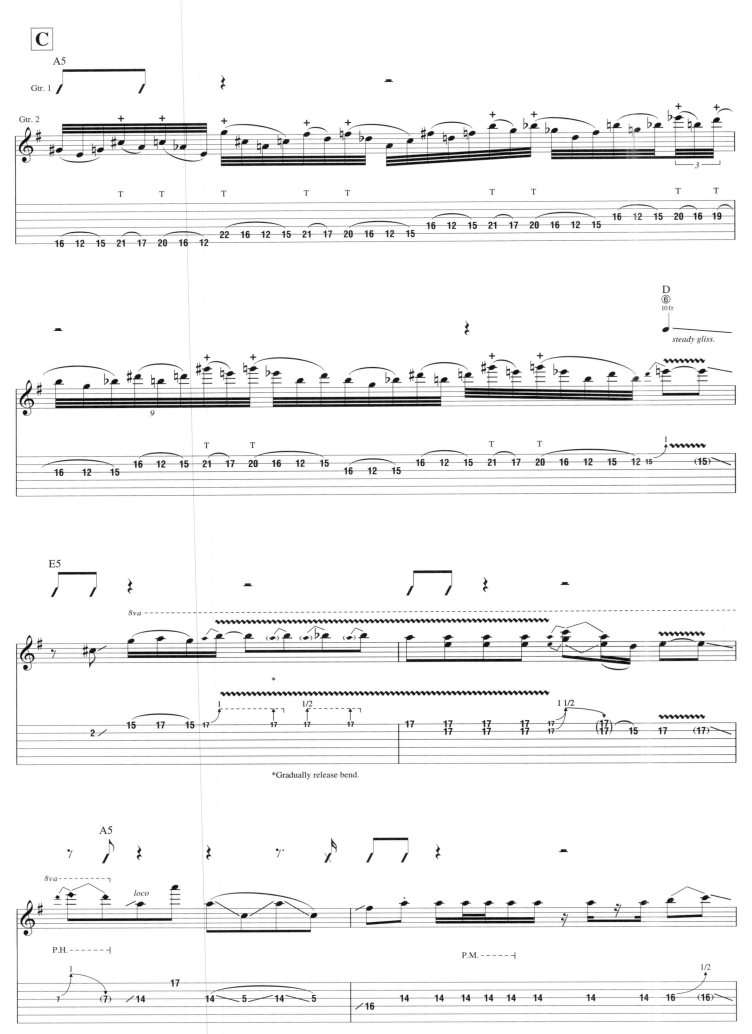

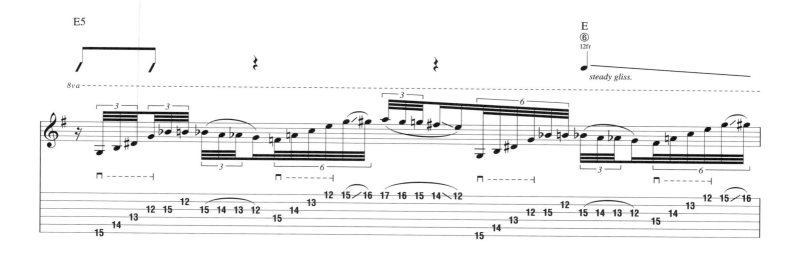

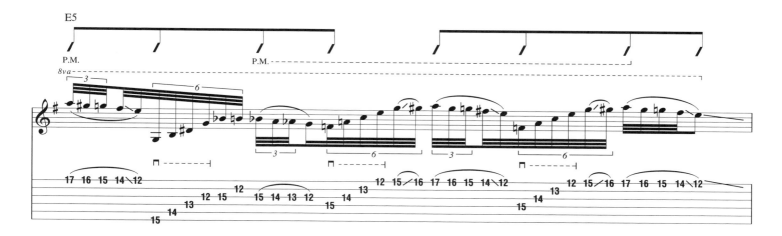

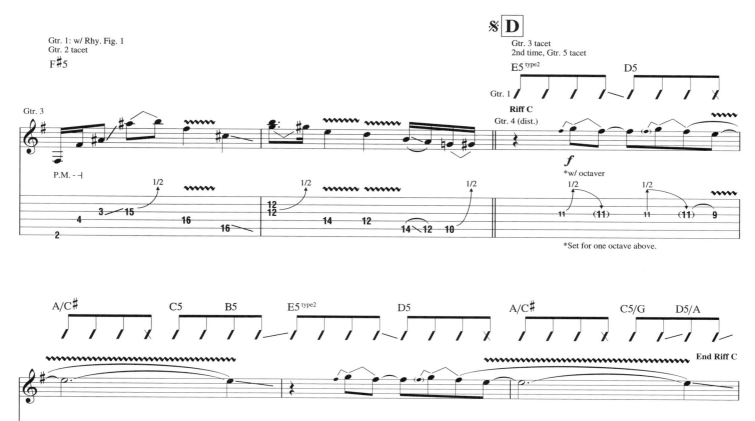

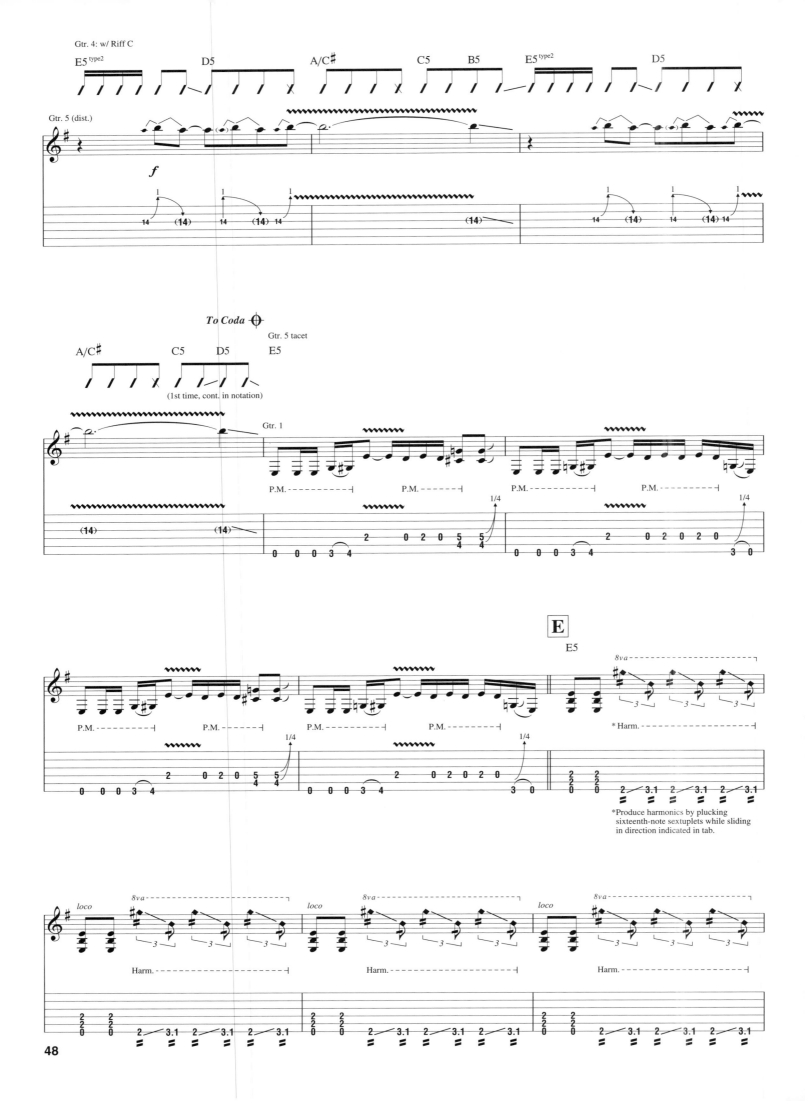

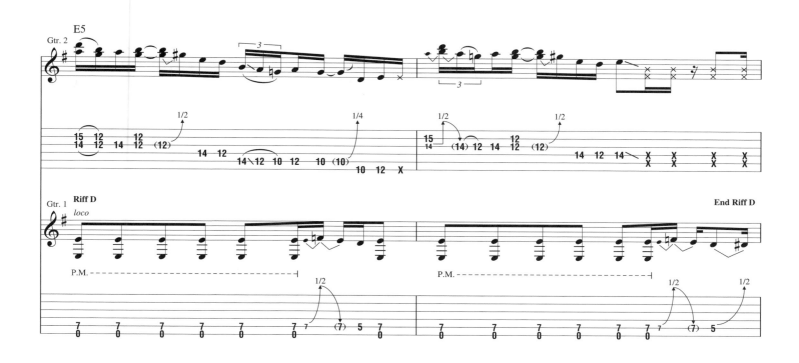

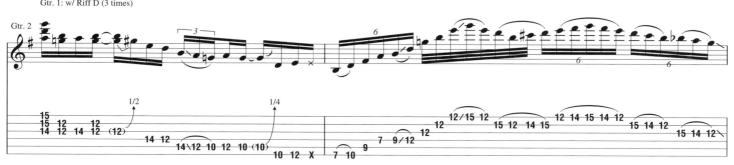

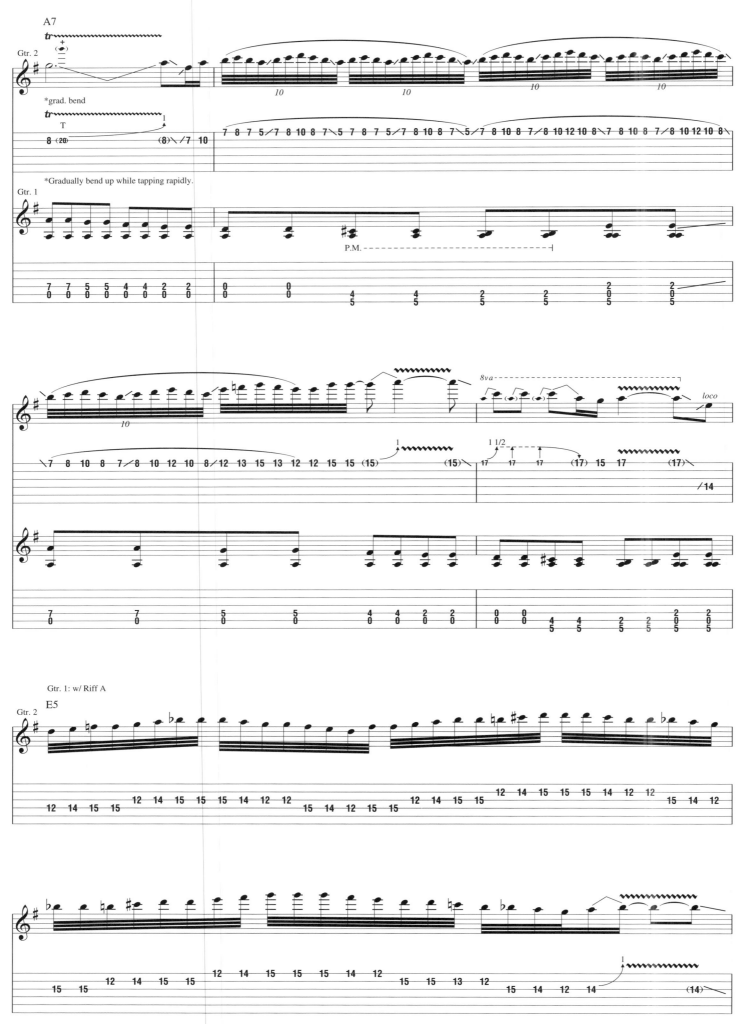

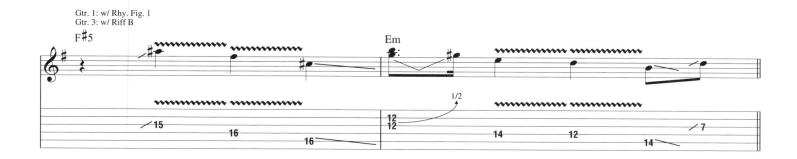

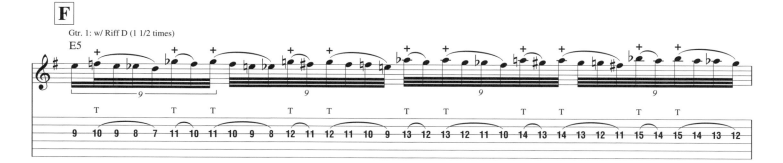

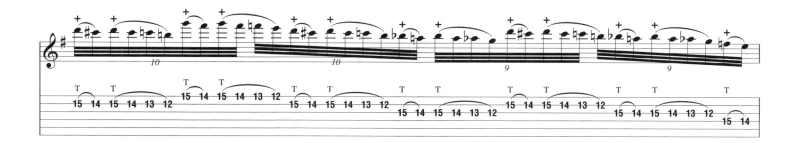

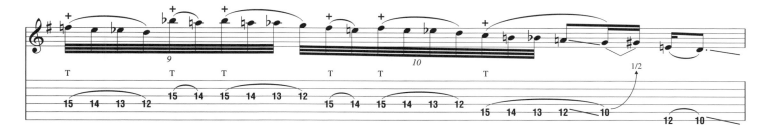

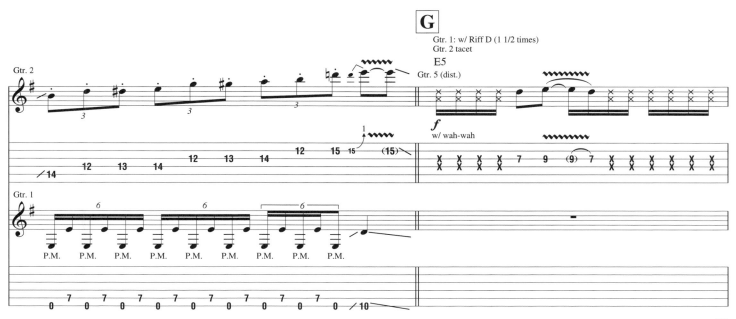

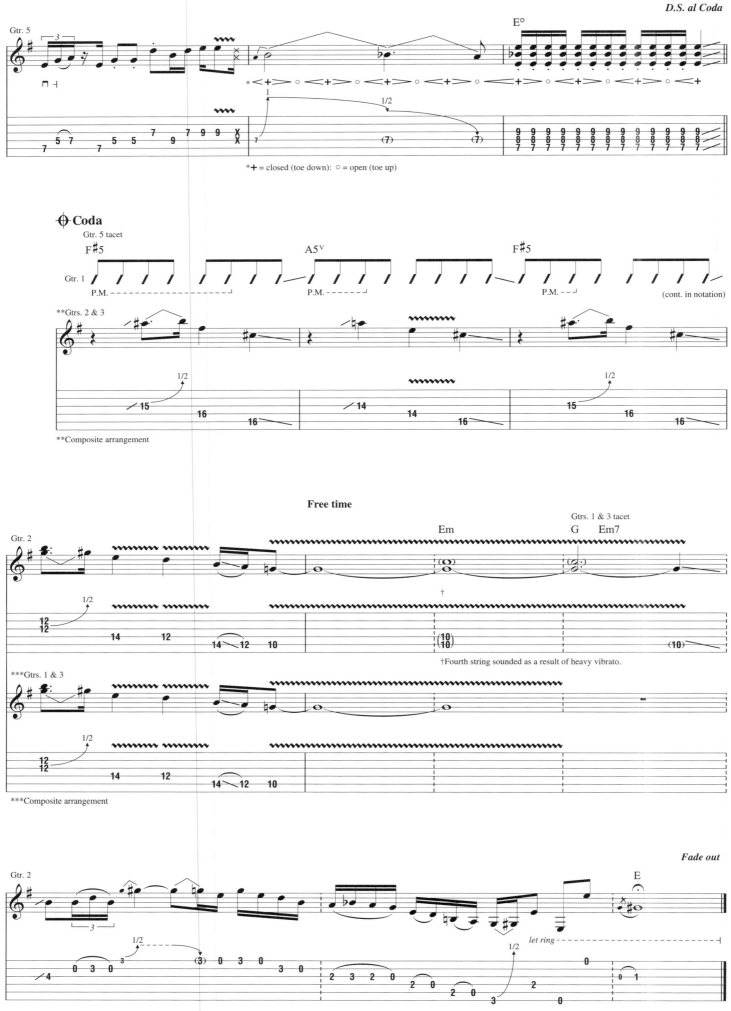

Fiddler's
Music by John 5

A

Very fast ♩ = 303

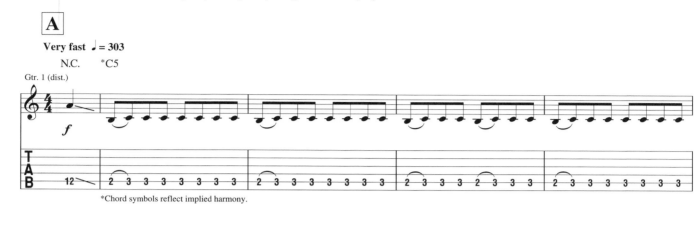

*Chord symbols reflect implied harmony.

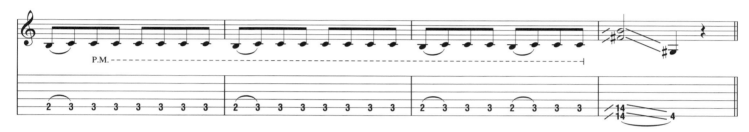

B

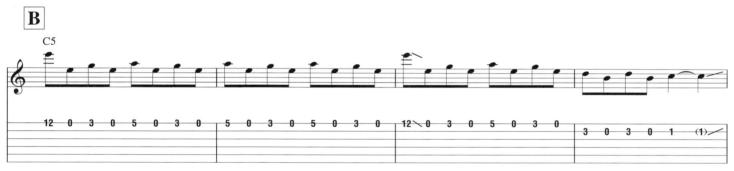

C

Gtr. 1 tacet

C5

F5

Gtr. 2 (dist.)

f

w/ wah-wah

sim.

* **+** = closed (toe down): ○ = open (toe up)

54

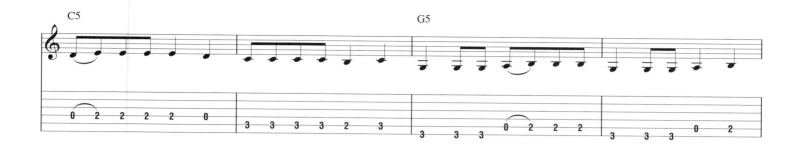

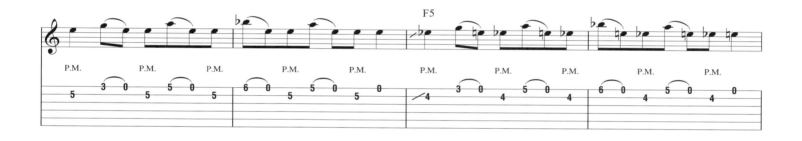

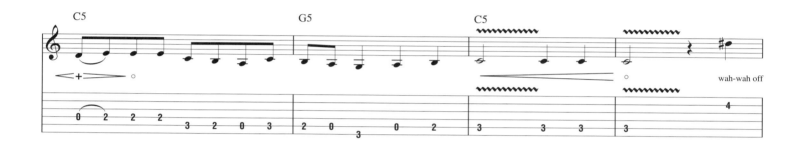

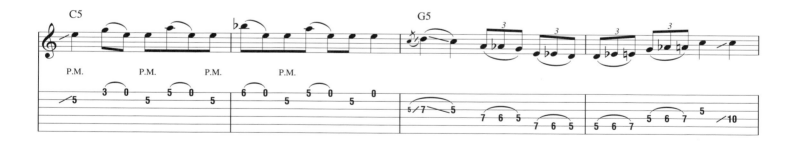

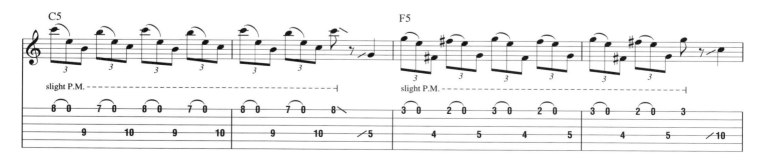

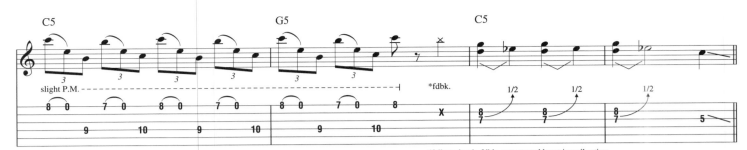

*Microphonic fdbk., not caused by string vibration.

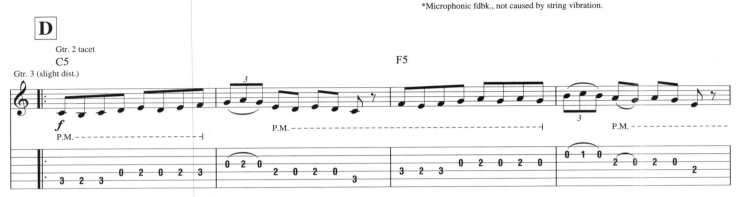

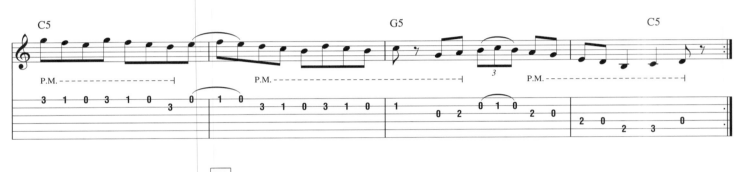

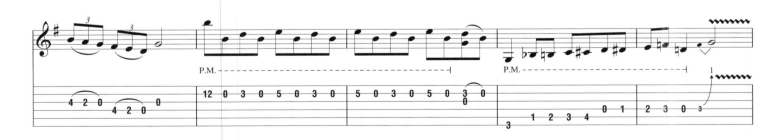

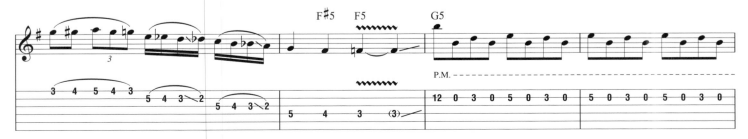

56

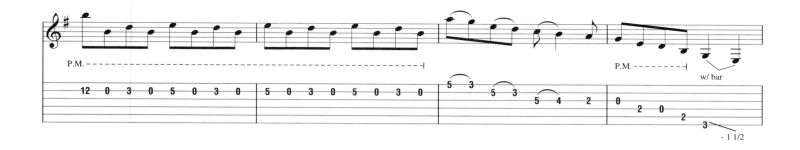

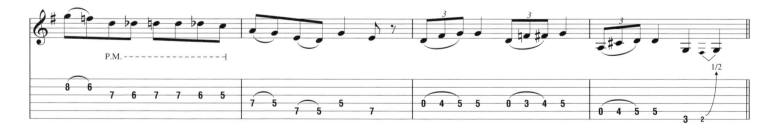

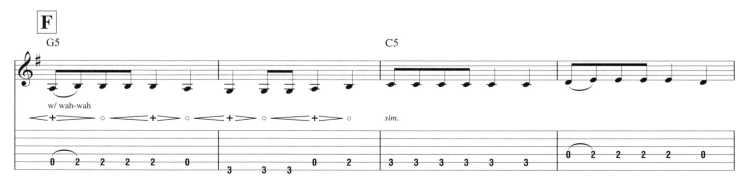

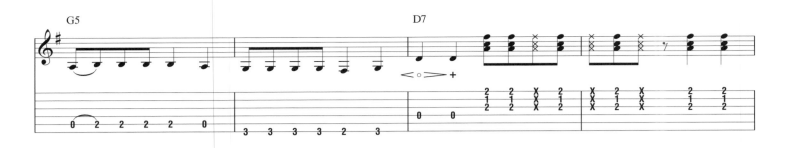

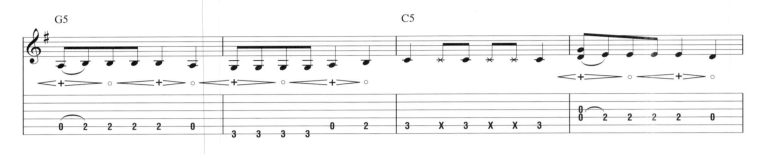

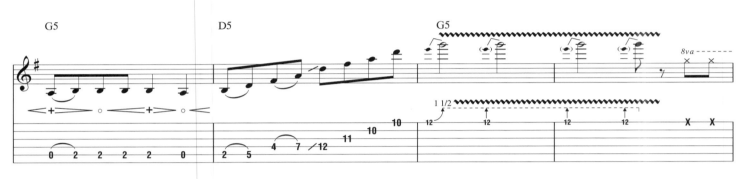

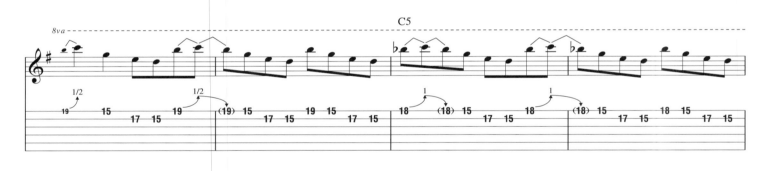

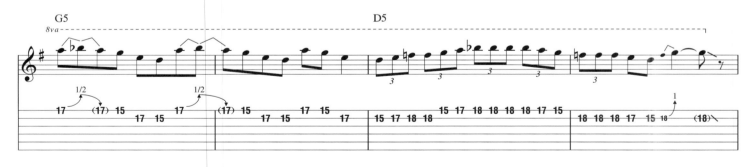

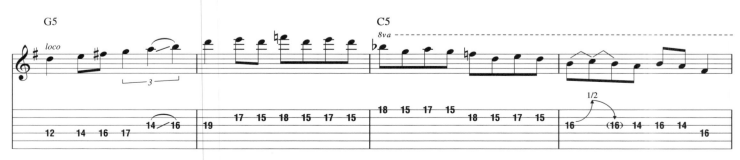

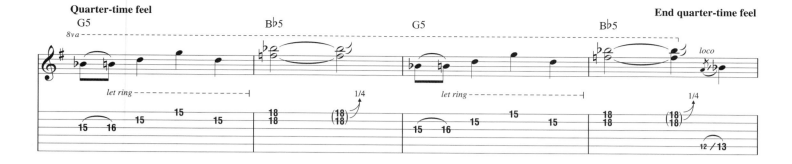

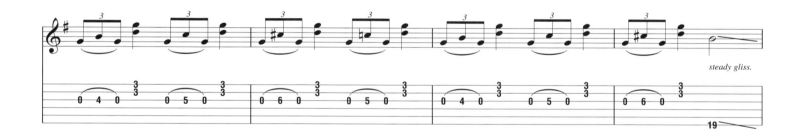

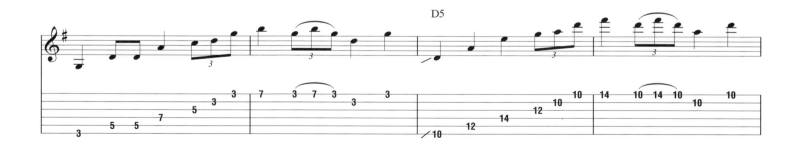

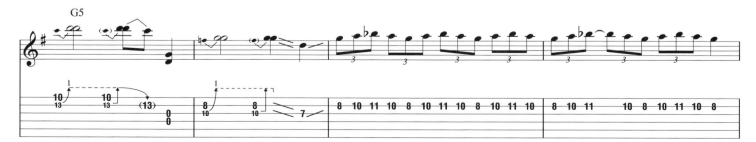

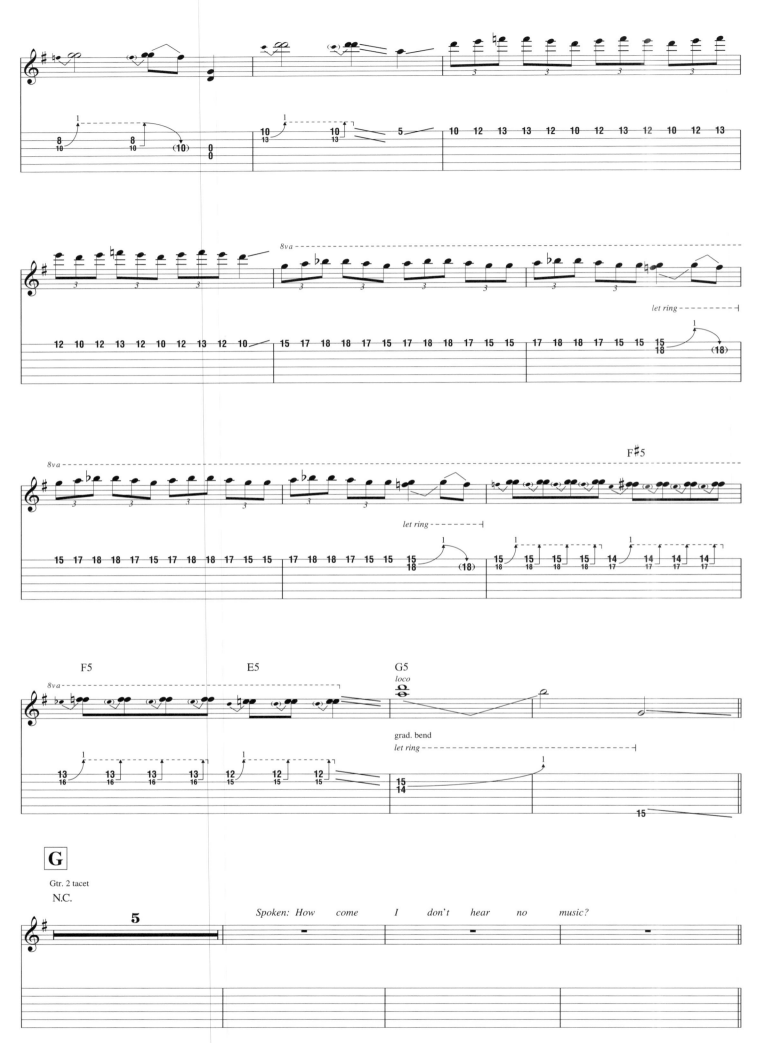

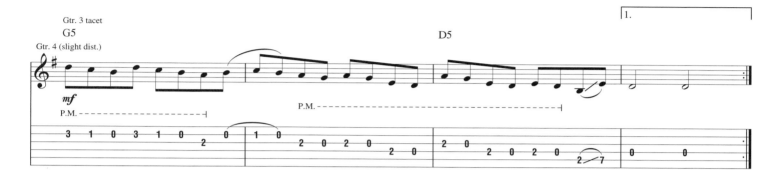

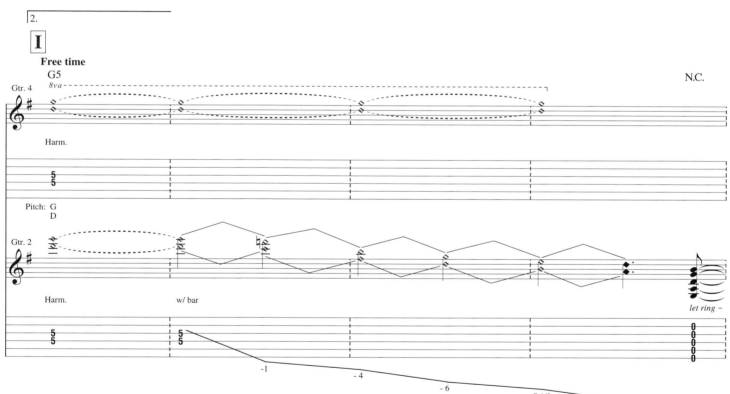

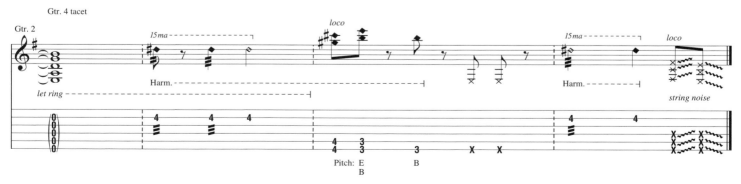

Gods and Monsters

Music by John 5

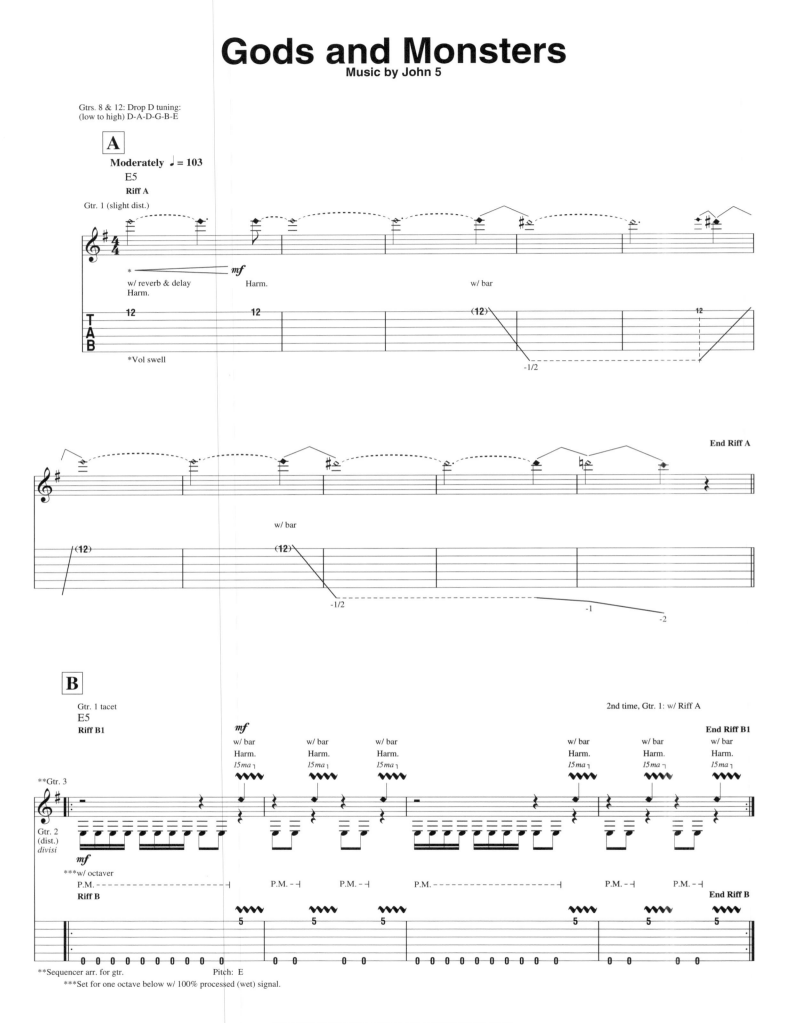

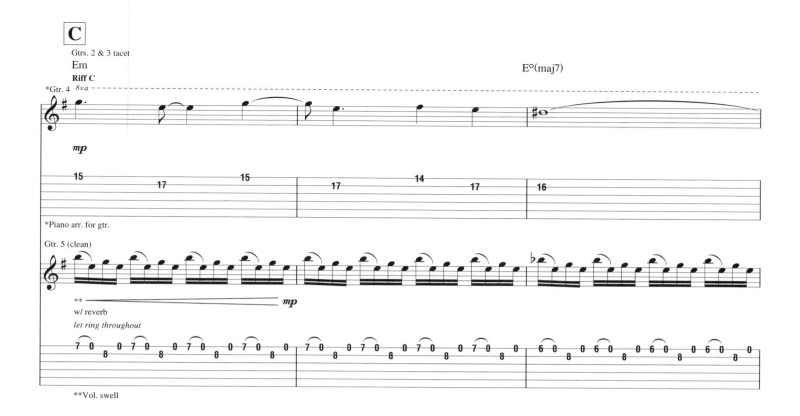

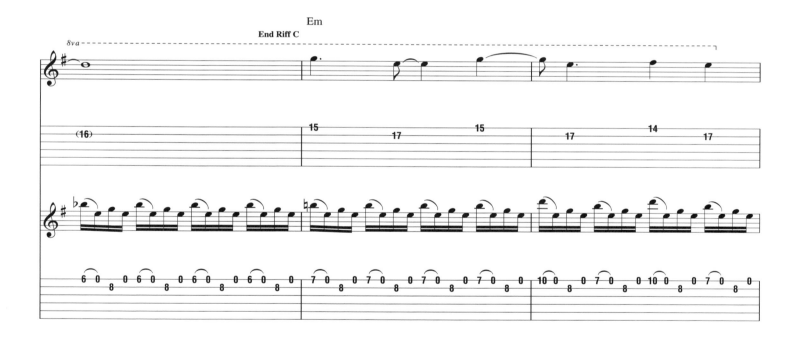

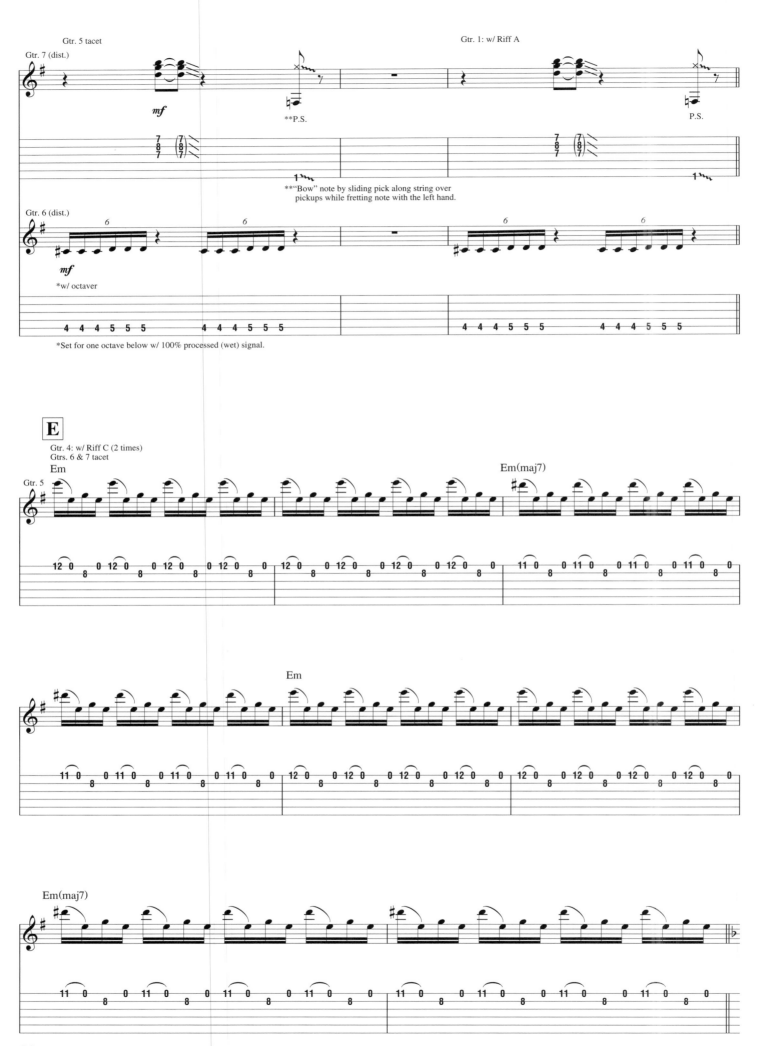

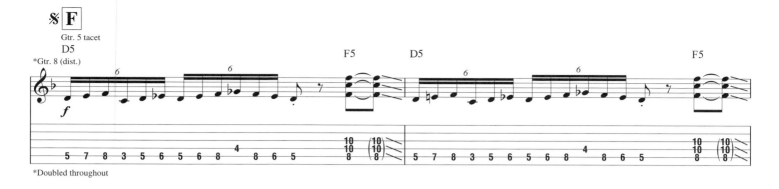

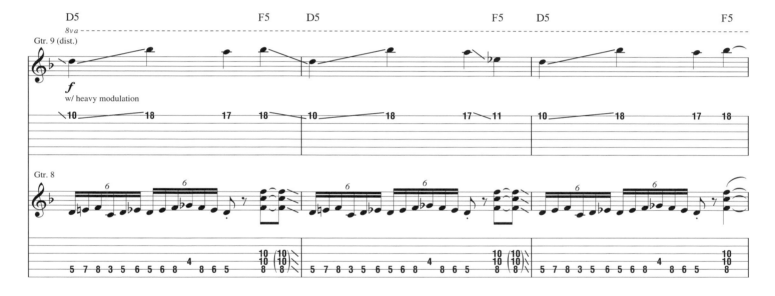

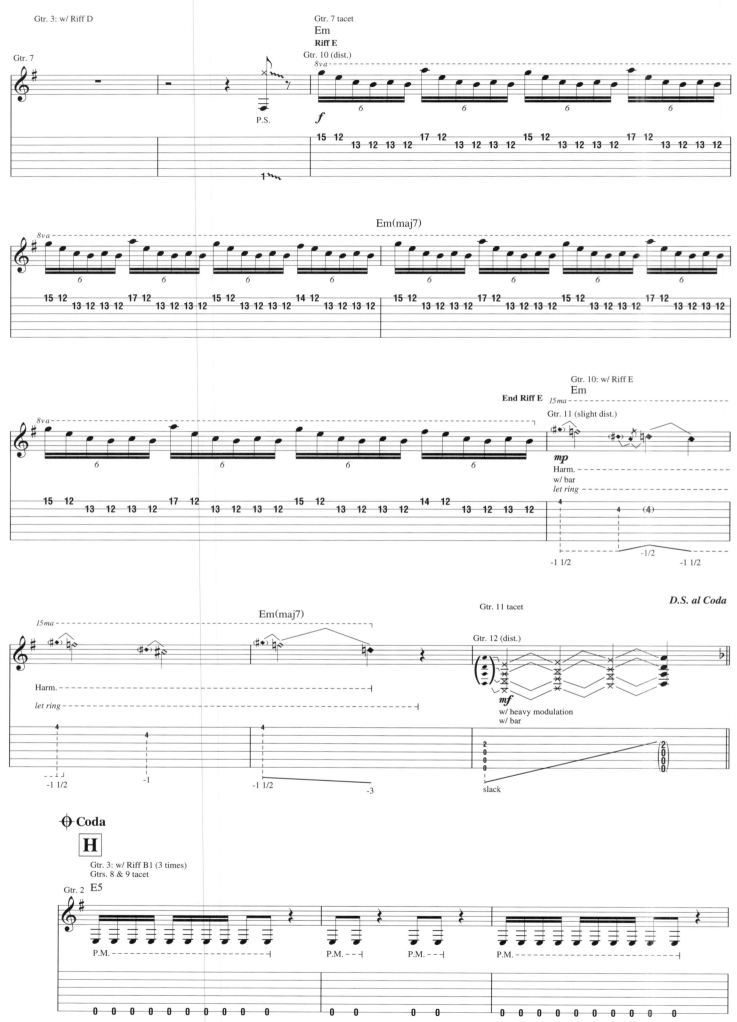

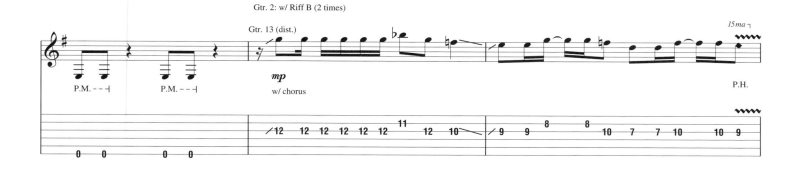

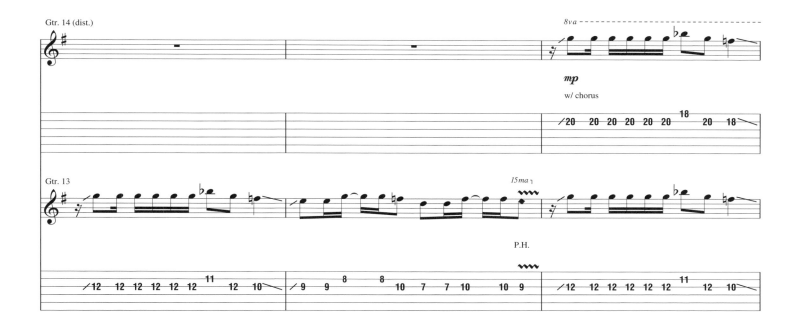

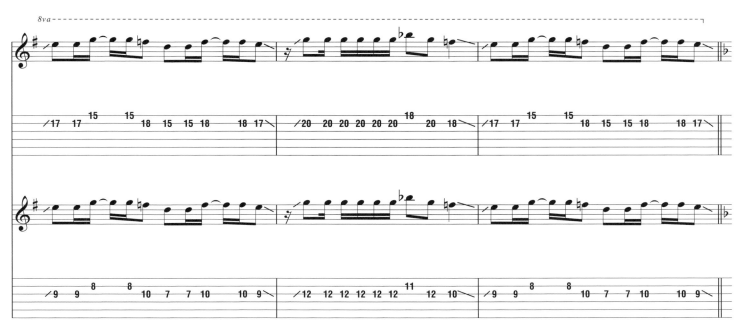

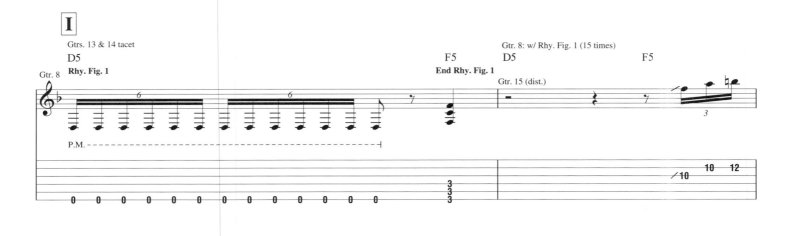

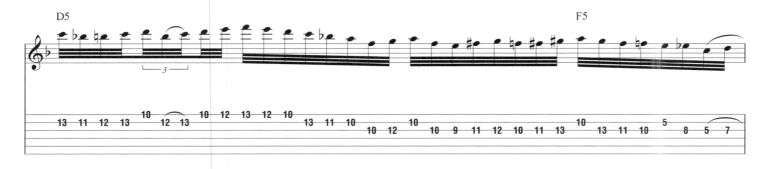

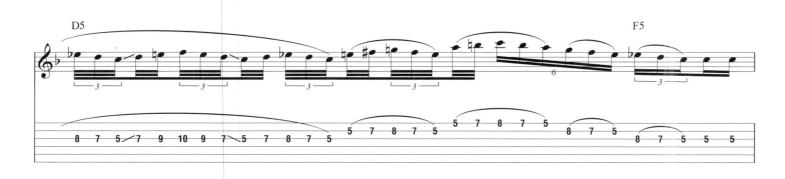

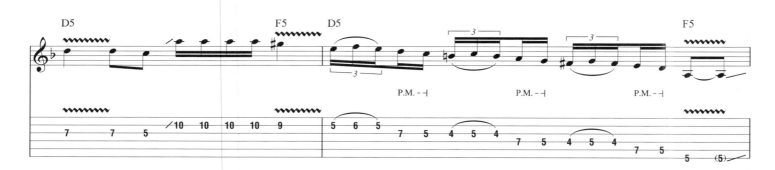

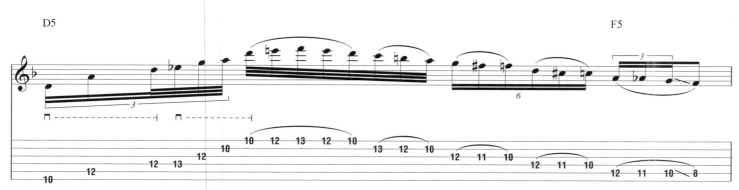

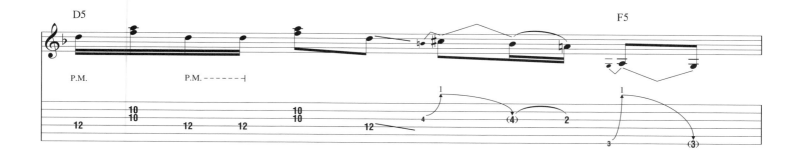

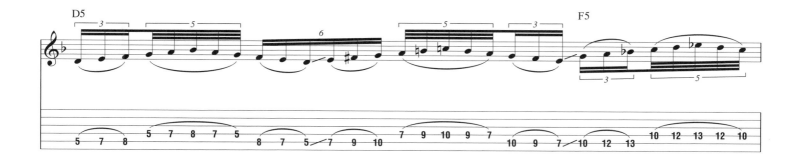

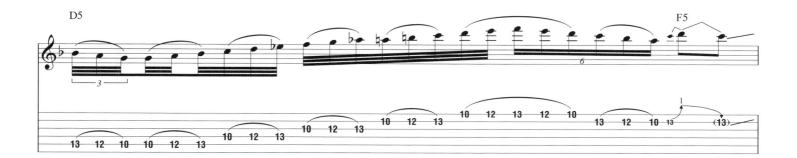

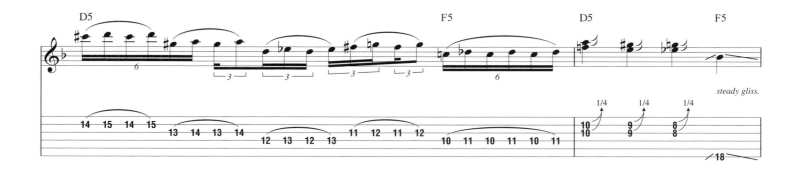

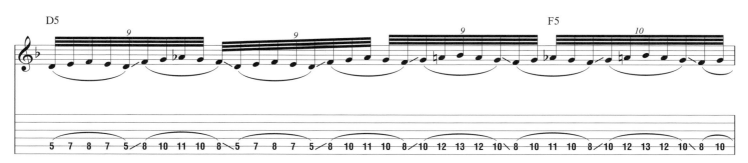

2 Die 4

Music by John 5 and Kevin Savigar

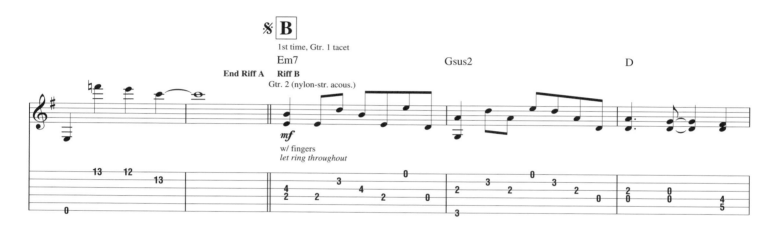

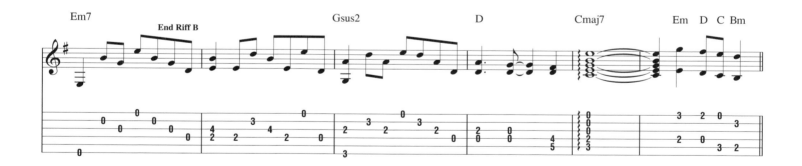

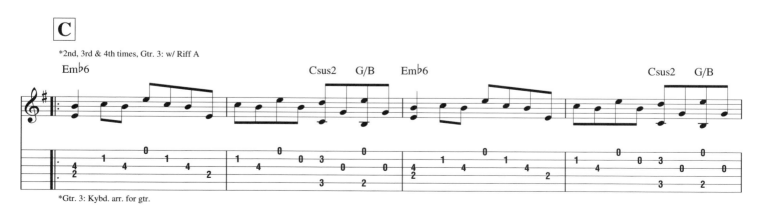

D

To Coda ⊕

D.S. al Coda
(take repeat)

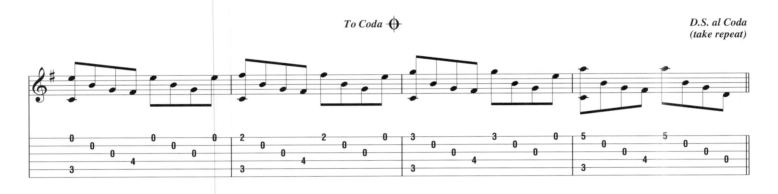

⊕ **Coda**

E

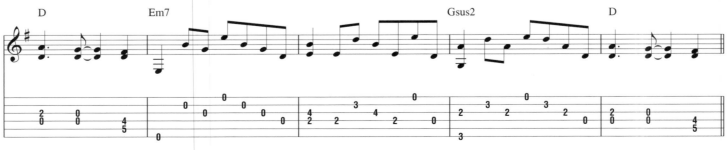

F

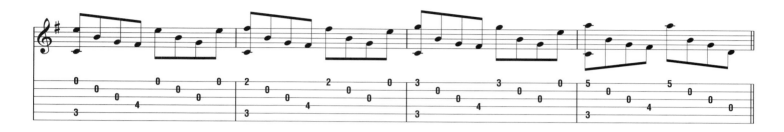

G

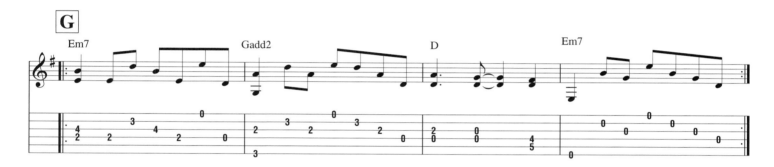

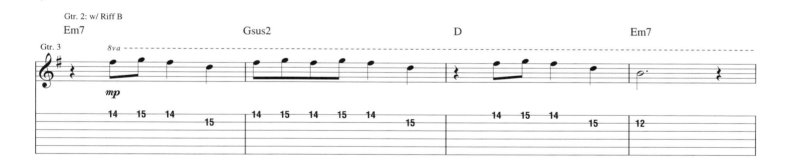

Death Valley

Music by John 5 and Kevin Savigar

D

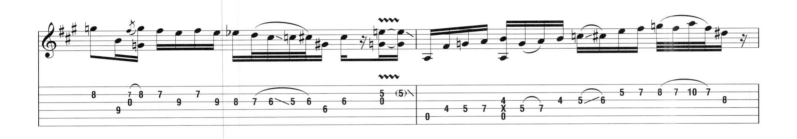

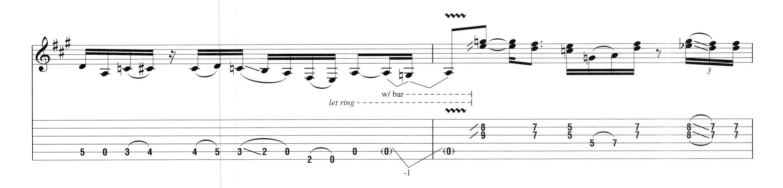

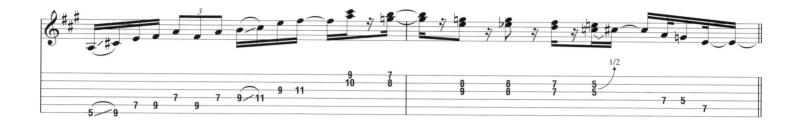

E

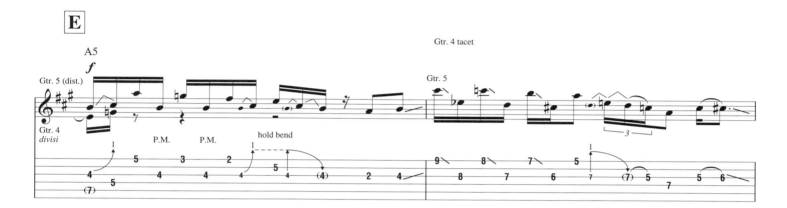

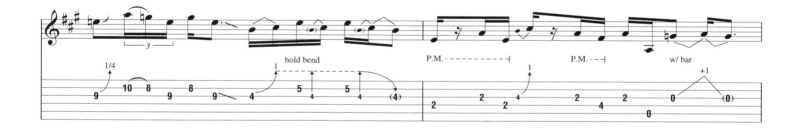

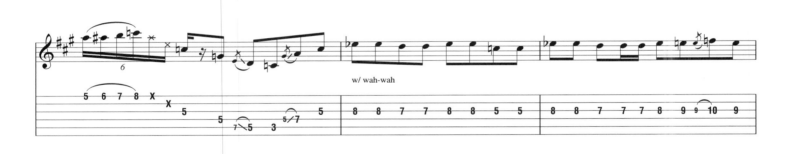

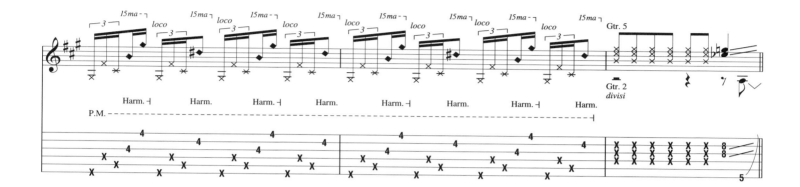

F

G

Gtr. 1: w/ Rhy. Fig. 1 (3 times)
Gtr. 2: w/ Riff A

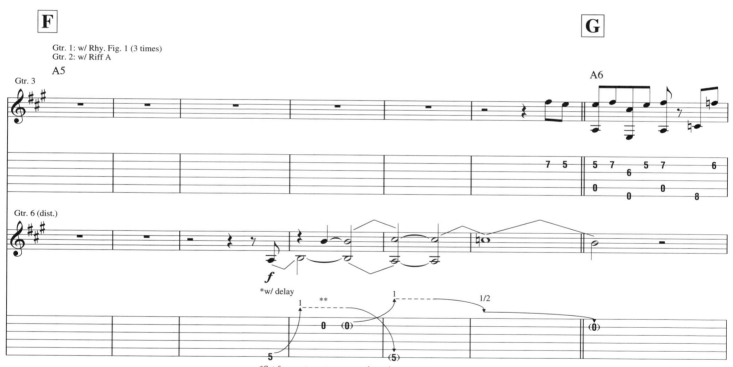

*Set for quarter-note regeneration w/ one repeat.
**Pick open string w/ ring finger of left hand while bending string w/ thumb of right hand behind the nut.

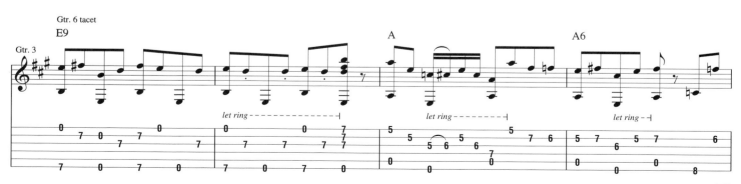

H

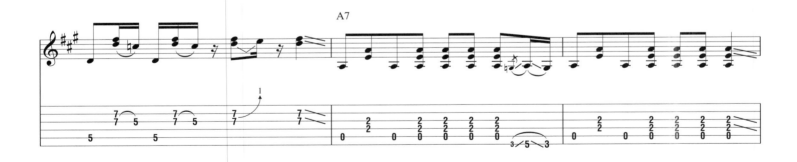

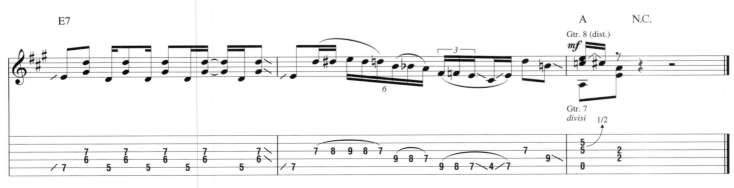

Perineum

Music by John 5

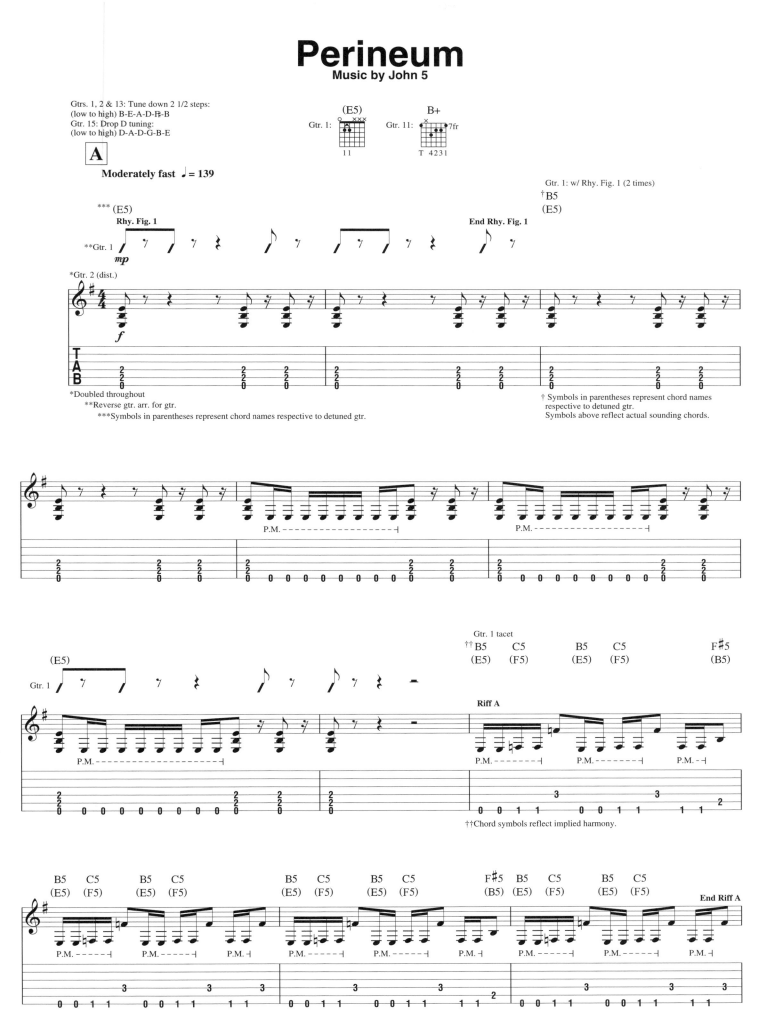

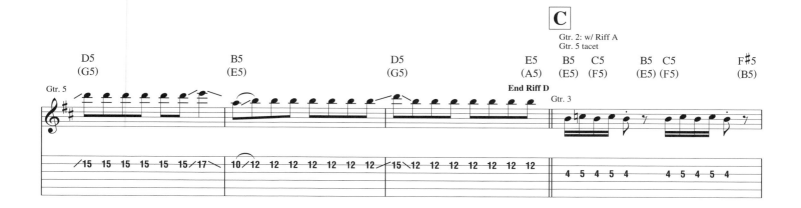

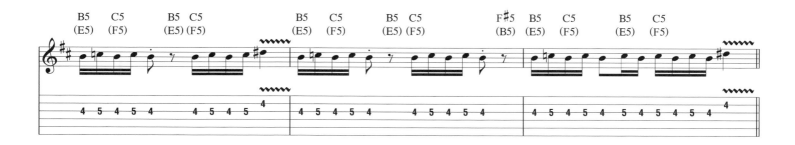

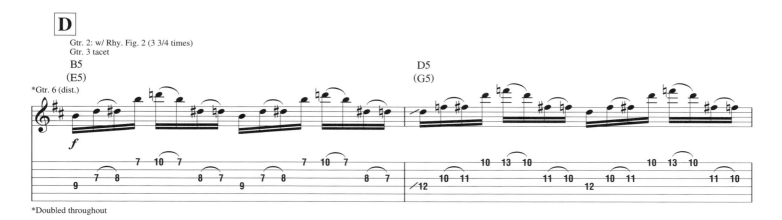

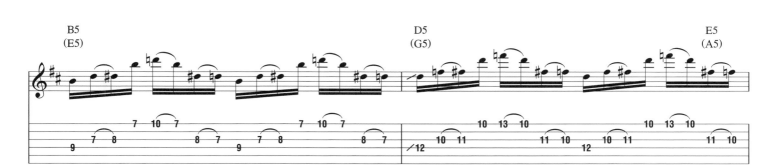

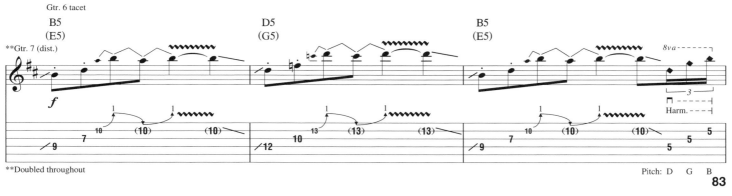

Pitch: D G B

83

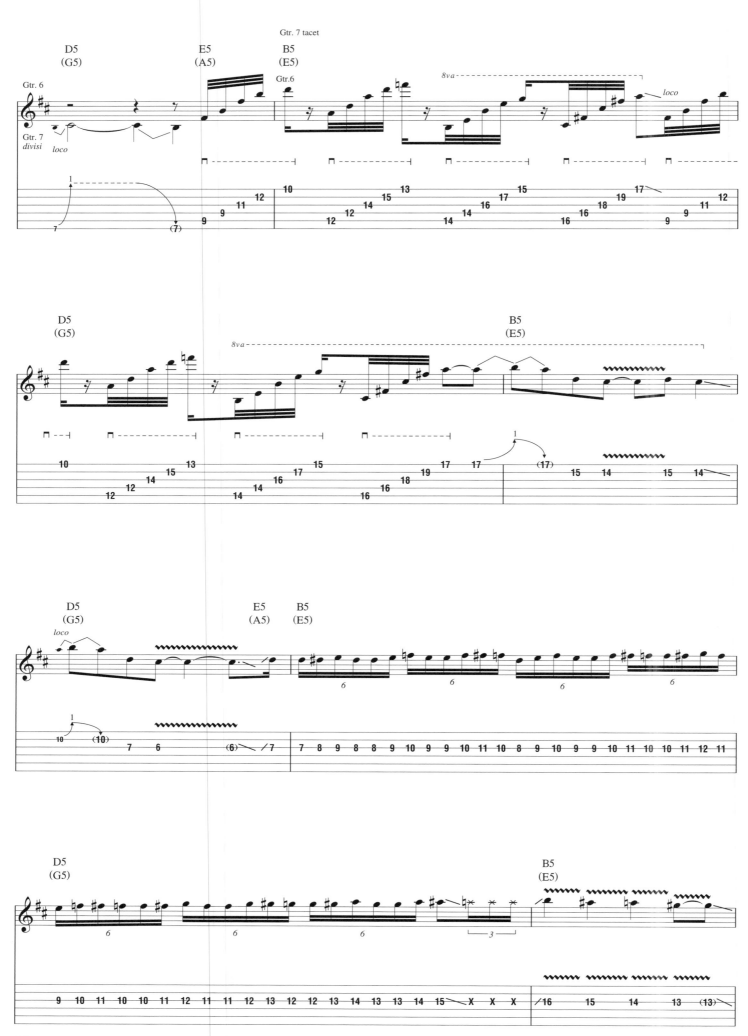

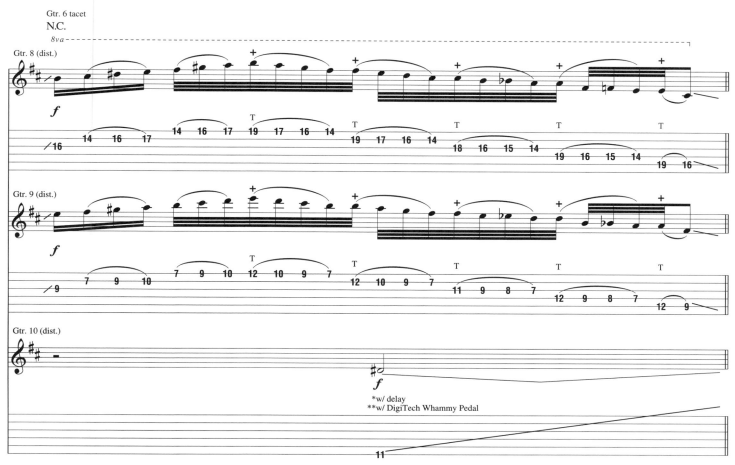

*w/ delay
**w/ DigiTech Whammy Pedal

*Delay set for quarter-note regeneration w/ two repeats.
**Whammy Pedal set for one octave above when depressed.

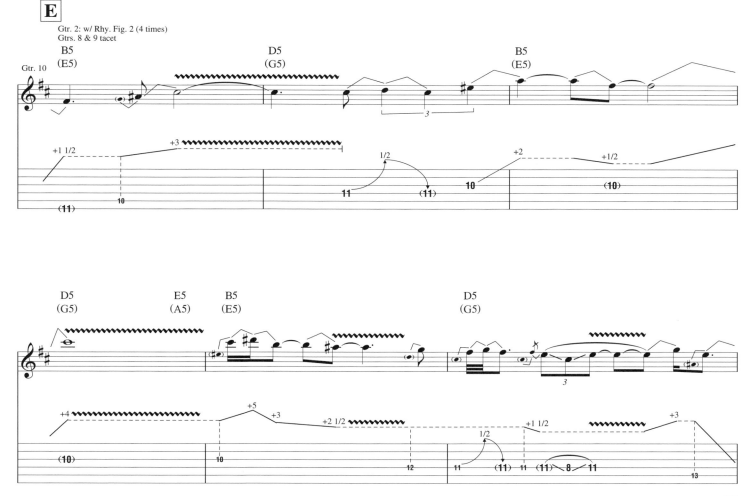

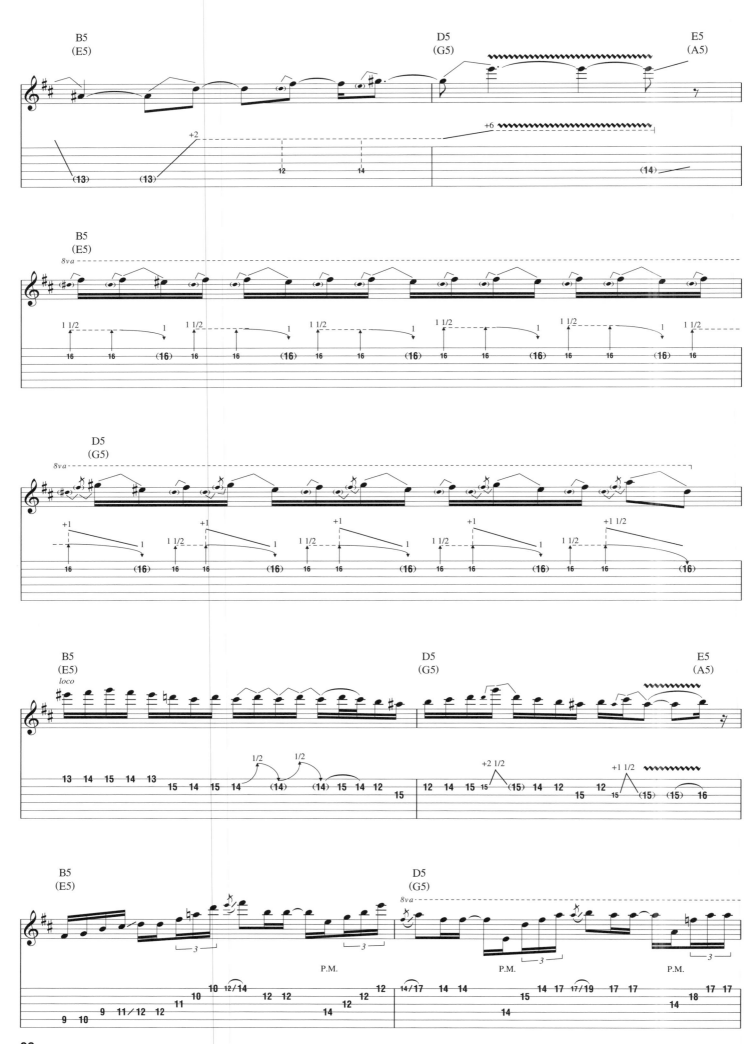

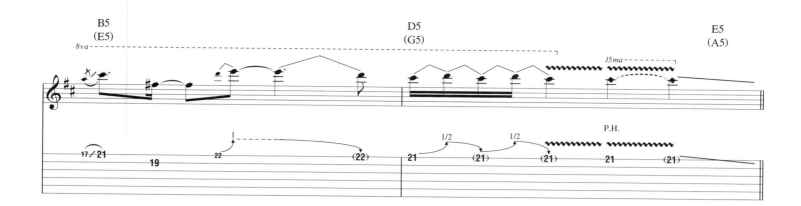

F

Gtr. 2: w/ Rhy. Fig. 2 (2 times)
Gtr. 4: w/ Riff C (2 times)
Gtr. 10 tacet

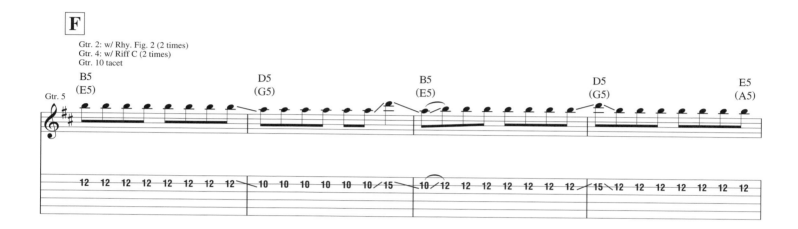

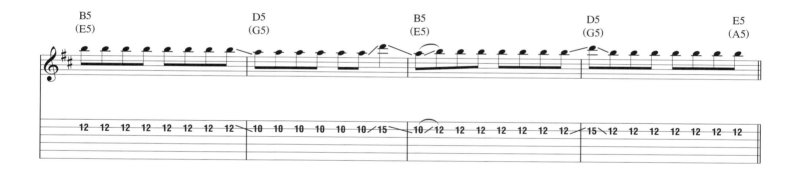

G

Gtr. 5: w/ Riff D (2 times)

B+

Rhy. Fig. 3

Rhy. Fig. 3A

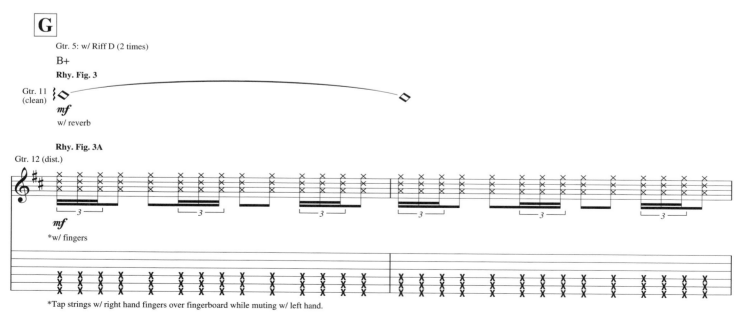

*Tap strings w/ right hand fingers over fingerboard while muting w/ left hand.

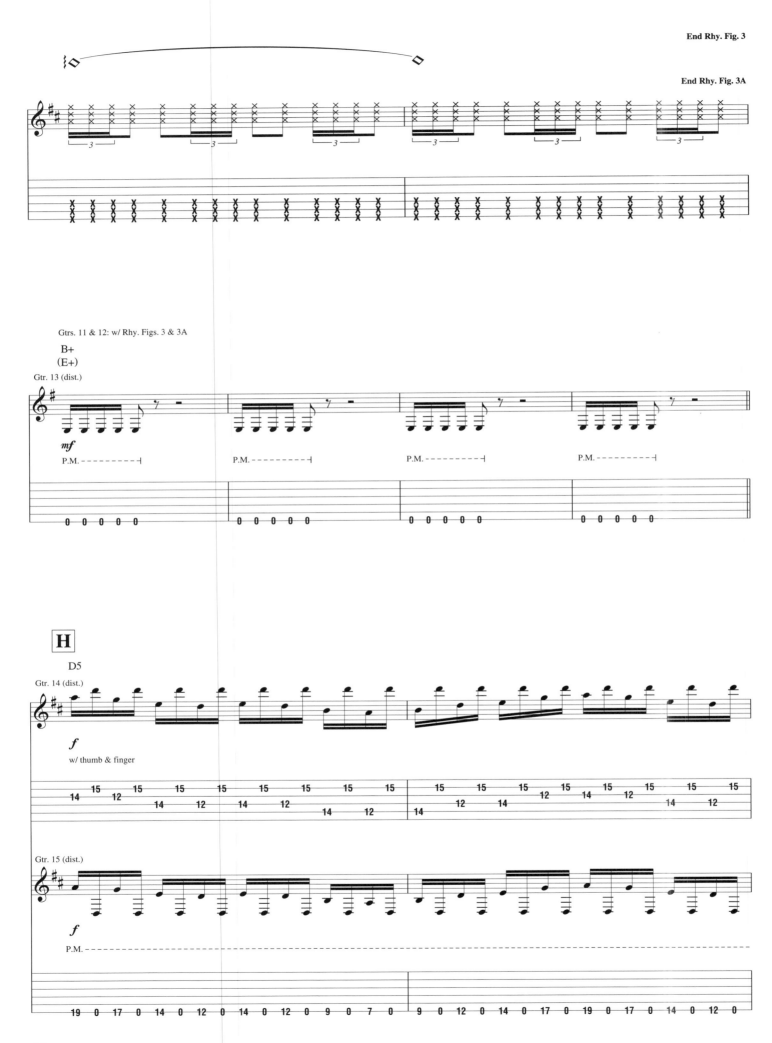

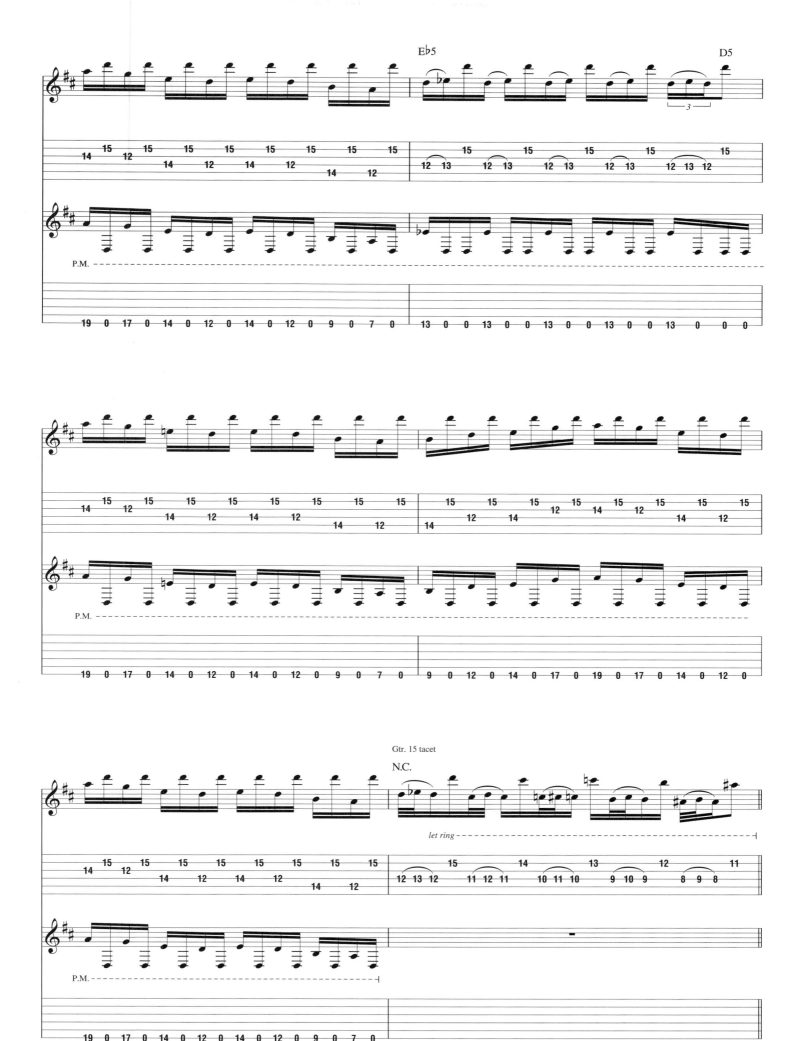

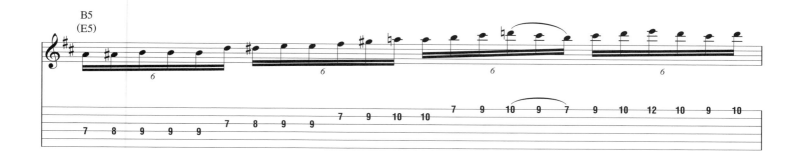

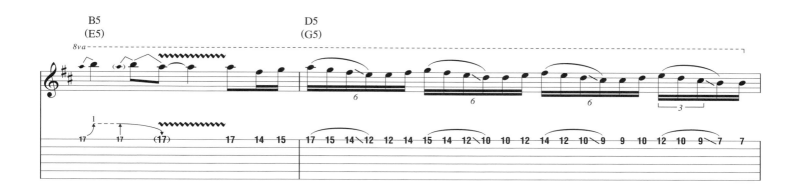

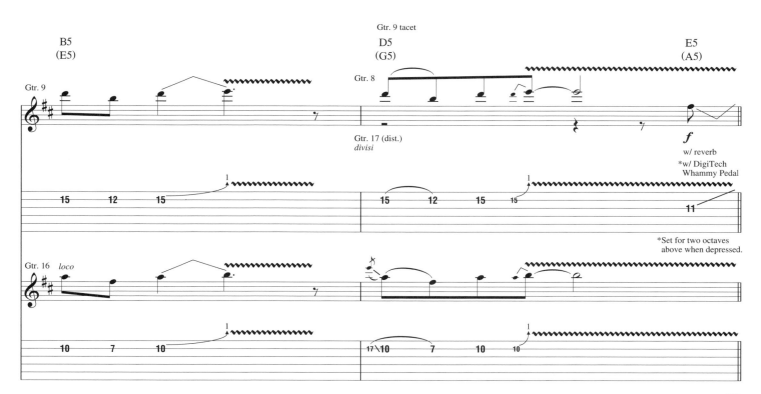

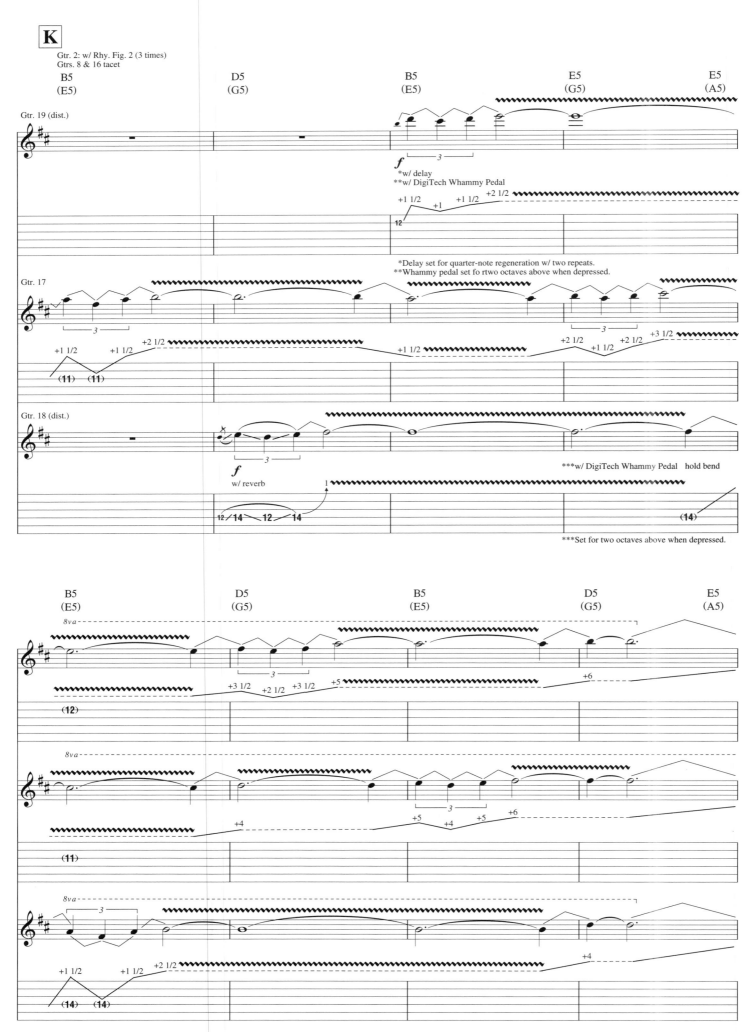

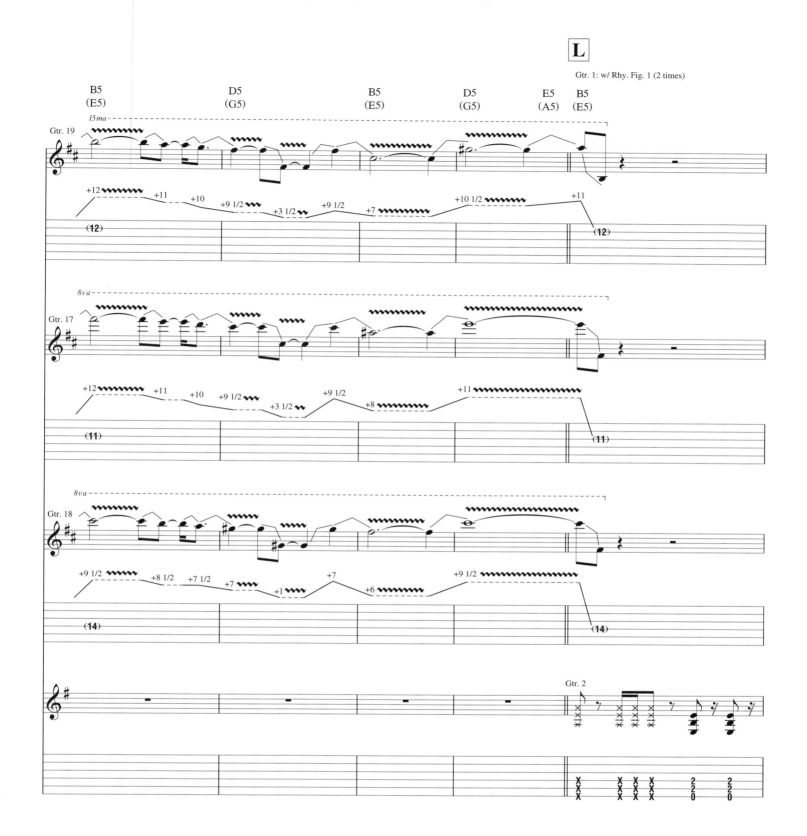

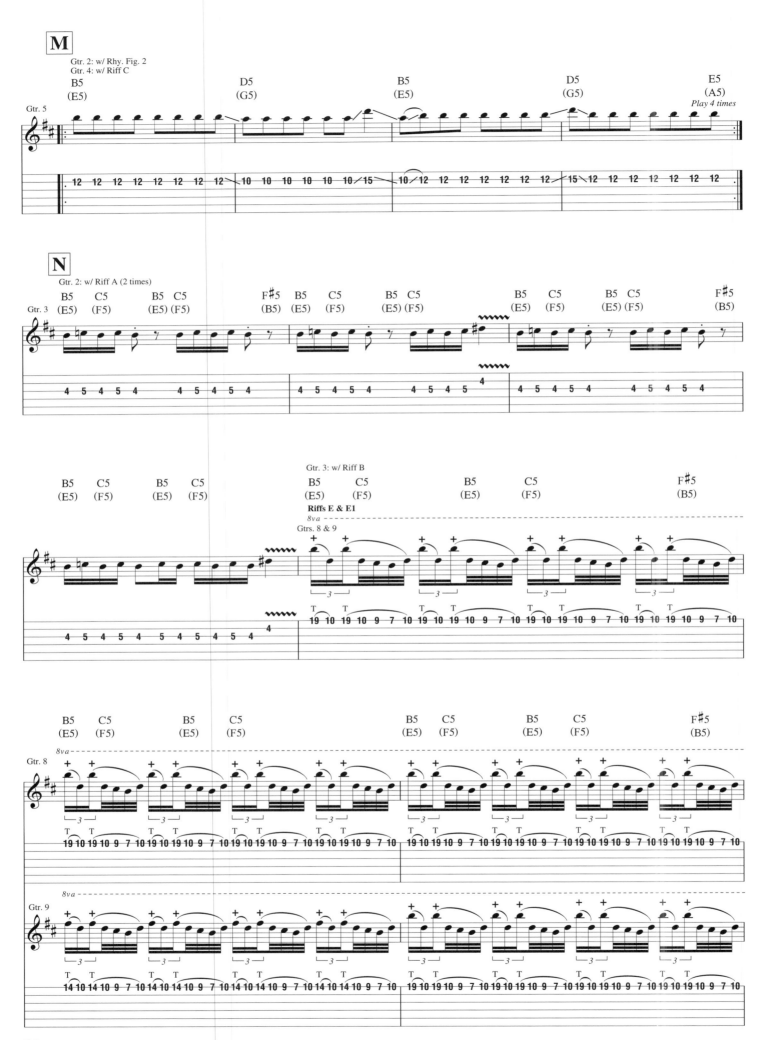

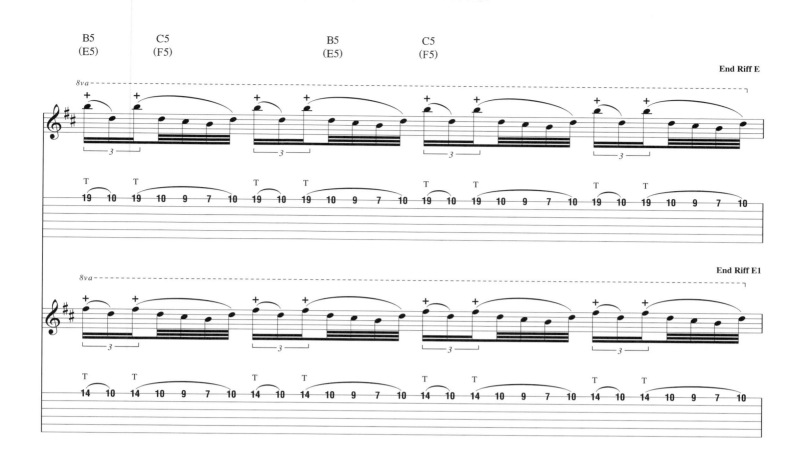

Gtrs. 8 & 9: w/ Riffs E & E1

O

Gtrs. 1 & 2 tacet
*Gtrs. 8 & 9: w/ Riffs E & E1 (1 3/4 times)

*Gradually fade out.

De'nouement
Music by John 5

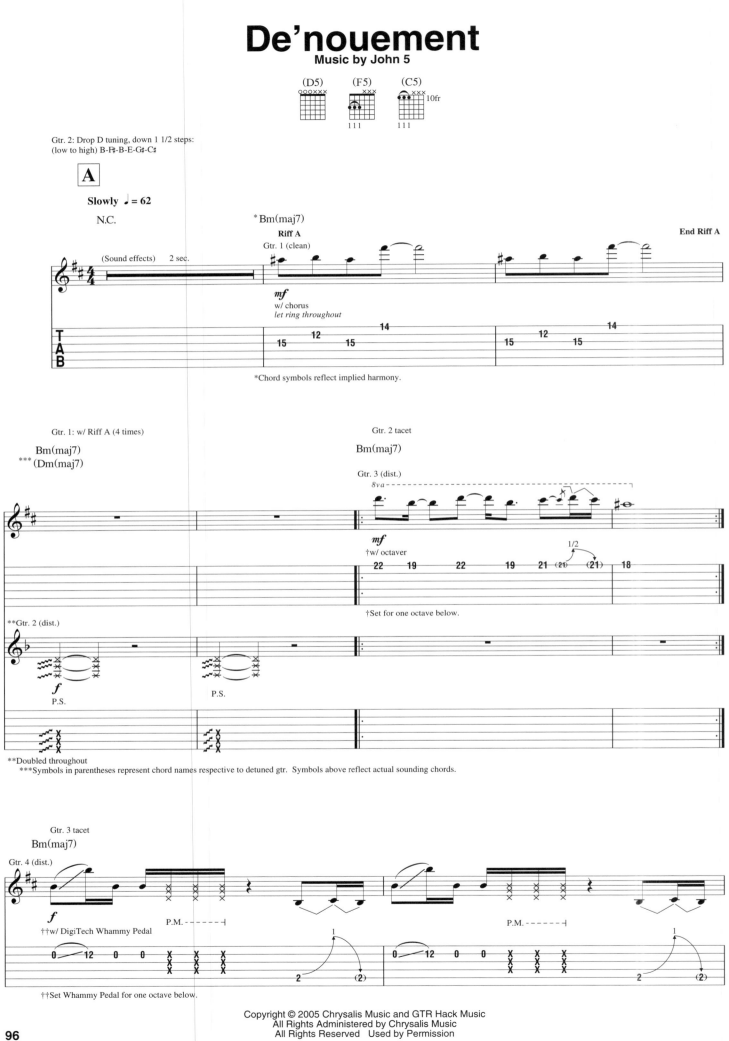

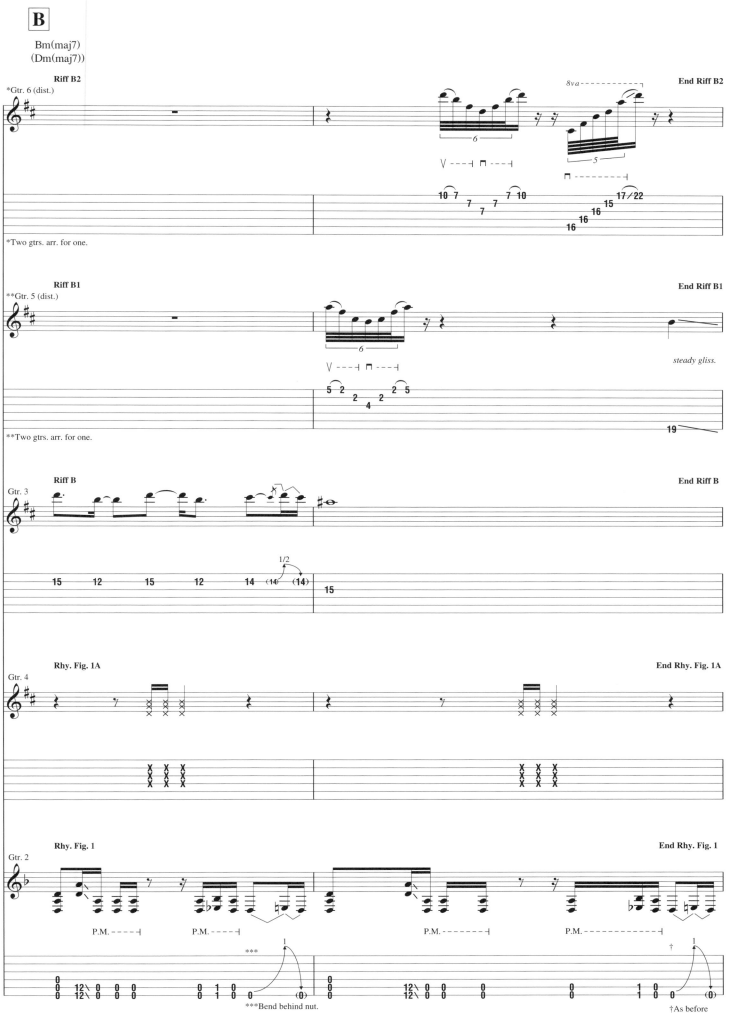

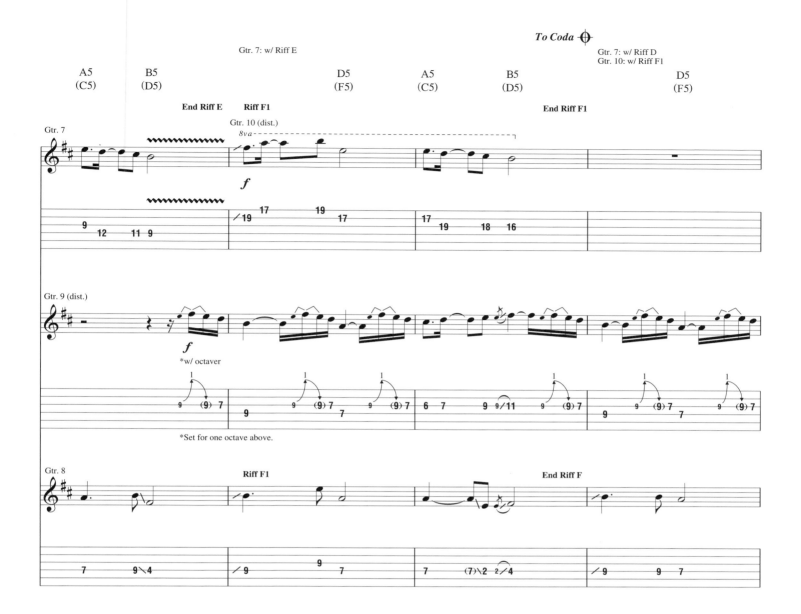

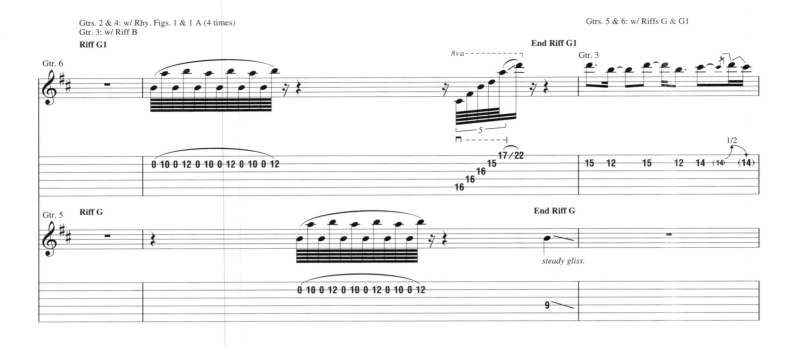

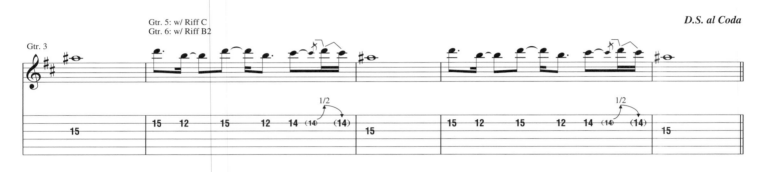

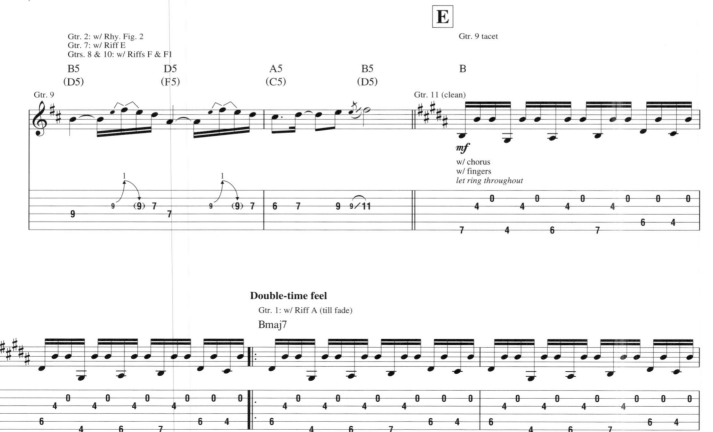

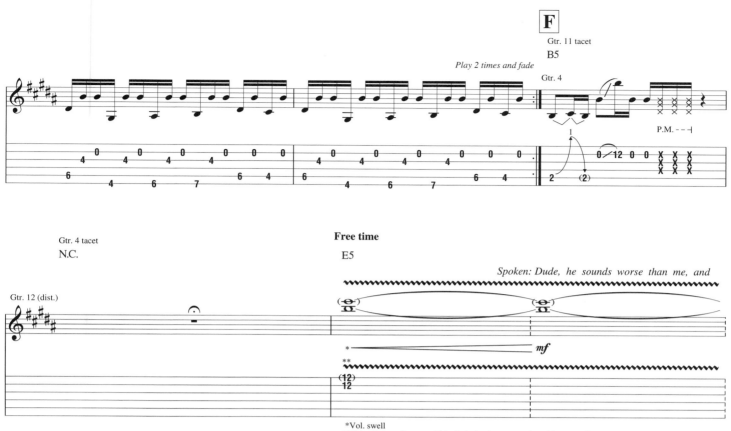

F

Gtr. 11 tacet

B5

Play 2 times and fade

Gtr. 4

P.M. - - -|

Gtr. 4 tacet

N.C.

Gtr. 12 (dist.)

Free time

E5

Spoken: Dude, he sounds worse than me, and

mf

*Vol. swell
**Using heavy vibrato, pull 1st & 2nd strings onto edge of frets, causing 1st string to sound.

I was like, oh, you know, "What time did you go to bed?" And he goes, "It's not that," and he goes, "I just, uh, nearly

died." And I'm like, immediately like, "What the hell happened?" He goes, "I was choking on a carrot." And he was in the other

room and couldn't hear me. And I'm like, "After all the crap you did, you're gonna buy it by choking on a carrot."

Guitar Notation Legend

Guitar Music can be notated three different ways: on a *musical staff*, in *tablature*, and in *rhythm slashes*.

RHYTHM SLASHES are written above the staff. Strum chords in the rhythm indicated. Use the chord diagrams found at the top of the first page of the transcription for the appropriate chord voicings. Round noteheads indicate single notes.

THE MUSICAL STAFF shows pitches and rhythms and is divided by bar lines into measures. Pitches are named after the first seven letters of the alphabet.

TABLATURE graphically represents the guitar fingerboard. Each horizontal line represents a a string, and each number represents a fret.

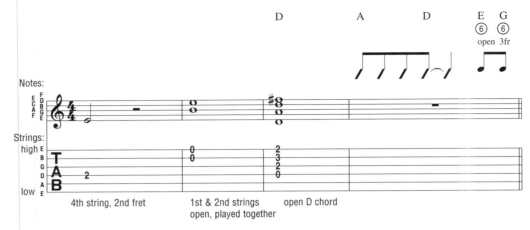

4th string, 2nd fret 1st & 2nd strings open, played together open D chord

Definitions for Special Guitar Notation

HALF-STEP BEND: Strike the note and bend up 1/2 step.

WHOLE-STEP BEND: Strike the note and bend up one step.

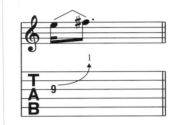

GRACE NOTE BEND: Strike the note and immediately bend up as indicated.

SLIGHT (MICROTONE) BEND: Strike the note and bend up 1/4 step.

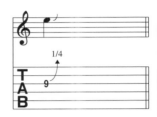

BEND AND RELEASE: Strike the note and bend up as indicated, then release back to the original note. Only the first note is struck.

PRE-BEND: Bend the note as indicated, then strike it.

PRE-BEND AND RELEASE: Bend the note as indicated. Strike it and release the bend back to the original note.

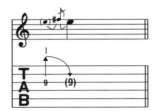

UNISON BEND: Strike the two notes simultaneously and bend the lower note up to the pitch of the higher.

VIBRATO: The string is vibrated by rapidly bending and releasing the note with the fretting hand.

WIDE VIBRATO: The pitch is varied to a greater degree by vibrating with the fretting hand.

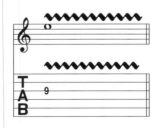

HAMMER-ON: Strike the first (lower) note with one finger, then sound the higher note (on the same string) with another finger by fretting it without picking.

PULL-OFF: Place both fingers on the notes to be sounded. Strike the first note and without picking, pull the finger off to sound the second (lower) note.

LEGATO SLIDE: Strike the first note and then slide the same fret-hand finger up or down to the second note. The second note is not struck.

SHIFT SLIDE: Same as legato slide, except the second note is struck.

TRILL: Very rapidly alternate between the notes indicated by continuously hammering on and pulling off.

TAPPING: Hammer ("tap") the fret indicated with the pick-hand index or middle finger and pull off to the note fretted by the fret hand.

NATURAL HARMONIC: Strike the note while the fret-hand lightly touches the string directly over the fret indicated.

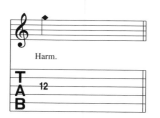

PINCH HARMONIC: The note is fretted normally and a harmonic is produced by adding the edge of the thumb or the tip of the index finger of the pick hand to the normal pick attack.

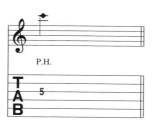

HARP HARMONIC: The note is fretted normally and a harmonic is produced by gently resting the pick hand's index finger directly above the indicated fret (in parentheses) while the pick hand's thumb or pick assists by plucking the appropriate string.

PICK SCRAPE: The edge of the pick is rubbed down (or up) the string, producing a scratchy sound.

MUFFLED STRINGS: A percussive sound is produced by laying the fret hand across the string(s) without depressing, and striking them with the pick hand.

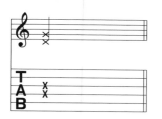

PALM MUTING: The note is partially muted by the pick hand lightly touching the string(s) just before the bridge.

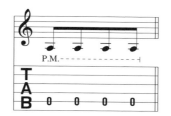

RAKE: Drag the pick across the strings indicated with a single motion.

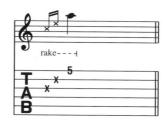

TREMOLO PICKING: The note is picked as rapidly and continuously as possible.

ARPEGGIATE: Play the notes of the chord indicated by quickly rolling them from bottom to top.

VIBRATO BAR DIVE AND RETURN: The pitch of the note or chord is dropped a specified number of steps (in rhythm) then returned to the original pitch.

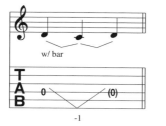

VIBRATO BAR SCOOP: Depress the bar just before striking the note, then quickly release the bar.

VIBRATO BAR DIP: Strike the note and then immediately drop a specified number of steps, then release back to the original pitch.

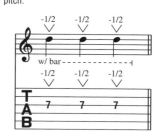

Additional Musical Definitions

(accent)	•	Accentuate note (play it louder)
(accent)	•	Accentuate note with great intensity
(staccato)	•	Play the note short
	•	Downstroke
V	•	Upstroke
D.S. al Coda	•	Go back to the sign (𝄋), then play until the measure marked "*To Coda*," then skip to the section labelled "**Coda**."
D.C. al Fine	•	Go back to the beginning of the song and play until the measure marked "***Fine***" (end).

Rhy. Fig.	•	Label used to recall a recurring accompaniment pattern (usually chordal).
Riff	•	Label used to recall composed, melodic lines (usually single notes) which recur.
Fill	•	Label used to identify a brief melodic figure which is to be inserted into the arrangement.
Rhy. Fill	•	A chordal version of a Fill.
tacet	•	Instrument is silent (drops out).
	•	Repeat measures between signs.
	•	When a repeated section has different endings, play the first ending only the first time and the second ending only the second time.

NOTE: Tablature numbers in parentheses mean:
1. The note is being sustained over a system (note in standard notation is tied), or
2. The note is sustained, but a new articulation (such as a hammer-on, pull-off, slide or vibrato begins), or
3. The note is a barely audible "ghost" note (note in standard notation is also in parentheses).

RECORDED VERSIONS
The Best Note-For-Note Transcriptions Available

ALL BOOKS INCLUDE TABLATURE

00690501 Adams, Bryan – Greatest Hits	$19.95
00692015 Aerosmith – Greatest Hits	$22.95
00690178 Alice in Chains – Acoustic	$19.95
00690387 Alice in Chains – Nothing Safe: The Best of the Box	$19.95
00694932 Allman Brothers Band – Volume 1	$24.95
00694933 Allman Brothers Band – Volume 2	$24.95
00690609 Audioslave	$19.95
00690366 Bad Company – Original Anthology, Book 1	$19.95
00690503 Beach Boys – Very Best of	$19.95
00690489 Beatles – 1	$24.95
00694929 Beatles – 1962-1966	$24.95
00694930 Beatles – 1967-1970	$24.95
00694832 Beatles – For Acoustic Guitar	$22.95
00690482 Beatles – Let It Be	$16.95
00690632 Beck – Sea Change	$19.95
00692385 Berry, Chuck	$19.95
00692200 Black Sabbath – We Sold Our Soul for Rock 'N' Roll	$19.95
00690674 Blink-182	$19.95
00690389 Blink-182 – Enema of the State	$19.95
00690523 Blink-182 – Take Off Your Pants & Jacket	$19.95
00690008 Bon Jovi – Cross Road	$19.95
00690491 Bowie, David – Best of	$19.95
00690451 Buckley, Jeff – Collection	$24.95
00690590 Clapton, Eric – Anthology	$29.95
00692391 Clapton, Eric – Best of, 2nd Edition	$22.95
00690415 Clapton Chronicles – Best of Eric Clapton	$18.95
00690074 Clapton, Eric – The Cream of Clapton	$24.95
00690716 Clapton, Eric – Me and Mr. Johnson	$19.95
00694869 Clapton, Eric – Unplugged	$22.95
00690162 Clash, Best of The	$19.95
00690682 Coldplay – Live 2003	$19.95
00690494 Coldplay – Parachutes	$19.95
00690593 Coldplay – A Rush of Blood to the Head	$19.95
00694940 Counting Crows – August & Everything After	$19.95
00690401 Creed – Human Clay	$19.95
00690352 Creed – My Own Prison	$19.95
00690551 Creed – Weathered	$19.95
00699521 Cure, The – Greatest Hits	$24.95
00690637 Dale, Dick – Best of	$19.95
00690289 Deep Purple, Best of	$17.95
00690384 Di Franco, Ani – Best of	$19.95
00690347 Doors, The – Anthology	$22.95
00690348 Doors, The – Essential Guitar Collection	$16.95
00690235 Foo Fighters – The Colour and the Shape	$19.95
00690595 Foo Fighters – One by One	$19.95
00690734 Franz Ferdinand	$19.95
00690222 G3 Live – Satriani, Vai, Johnson	$22.95
00120167 Godsmack	$19.95
00690338 Goo Goo Dolls – Dizzy Up the Girl	$19.95
00690601 Good Charlotte – The Young and the Hopeless	$19.95
00690591 Griffin, Patty – Guitar Collection	$19.95
00694798 Harrison, George – Anthology	$19.95
00692930 Hendrix, Jimi – Are You Experienced?	$24.95
00692931 Hendrix, Jimi – Axis: Bold As Love	$22.95
00690017 Hendrix, Jimi – Live at Woodstock	$24.95
00690602 Hendrix, Jimi – Smash Hits	$19.95
00690688 Incubus – A Crow Left of the Murder	$19.95
00690457 Incubus – Make Yourself	$19.95
00690544 Incubus – Morningview	$19.95
00690652 Jane's Addiction – Best of	$19.95
00690721 Jet – Get Born	$19.95
00690751 John5 – Vertigo	$19.95
00690660 Johnson, Eric – Best of	$19.95

00690271 Johnson, Robert – New Transcriptions	$24.95
00699131 Joplin, Janis – Best of	$19.95
00690651 Juanes – Exitos de Juanes	$19.95
00690427 Judas Priest – Best of	$19.95
00690742 Killers, The – Hot Fuss	$19.95
00690444 King, B.B. and Eric Clapton – Riding with the King	$19.95
00690157 Kiss – Alive	$19.95
00694903 Kiss – Best of	$24.95
00690156 Kiss	$17.95
00690658 Lang, Johnny – Long Time Coming	$19.95
00690614 Lavigne, Avril – Let Go	$19.95
00690726 Lavigne, Avril – Under My Skin	$19.95
00690743 Los Lonely Boys	$19.95
00690720 Lostprophets – Start Something	$19.95
00690525 Lynch, George – Best of	$19.95
00690577 Malmsteen, Yngwie – Anthology	$24.95
00694956 Marley, Bob – Legend	$19.95
00690548 Marley, Bob – One Love: Very Best of	$19.95
00694945 Marley, Bob – Songs of Freedom	$24.95
00690748 Maroon5 – 1.22.03 Acoustic	$19.95
00690657 Maroon5 – Songs About Jane	$19.95
00690616 Matchbox 20 – More Than You Think You Are	$19.95
00690239 Matchbox 20 – Yourself or Someone Like You	$19.95
00690382 McLachlan, Sarah – Mirrorball	$19.95
00120080 McLean, Don – Songbook	$19.95
00694952 Megadeth – Countdown to Extinction	$19.95
00694951 Megadeth – Rust in Peace	$22.95
00690505 Mellencamp, John – Guitar Collection	$19.95
00690562 Metheny, Pat – Bright Size Life	$19.95
00690559 Metheny, Pat – Question and Answer	$19.95
00690565 Metheny, Pat – Rejoicing	$19.95
00690040 Miller, Steve, Band – Young Hearts	$19.95
00690103 Morissette, Alanis – Jagged Little Pill	$19.95
00690722 New Found Glory – Catalyst	$19.95
00690611 Nirvana	$22.95
00690189 Nirvana – From the Muddy Banks of the Wishkah	$19.95
00694913 Nirvana – In Utero	$19.95
00694883 Nirvana – Nevermind	$19.95
00690026 Nirvana – Unplugged in New York	$19.95
00690739 No Doubt – Rock Steady	$22.95
00120112 No Doubt – Tragic Kingdom	$22.95
00690358 Offspring, The – Americana	$19.95
00690663 Offspring, The – Splinter	$19.95
00694847 Osbourne, Ozzy – Best of	$22.95
00690399 Osbourne, Ozzy – Ozzman Cometh	$19.95
00690594 Paul, Les – Best of	$19.95
00694855 Pearl Jam – Ten	$19.95
00690439 Perfect Circle, A – Mer De Noms	$19.95
00690661 Perfect Circle, A – Thirteenth Step	$19.95
00690499 Petty, Tom – The Definitive Guitar Collection	$19.95
00690240 Phish – Hoist	$19.95
00690731 Pillar – Where Do We Go from Here?	$19.95
00690428 Pink Floyd – Dark Side of the Moon	$19.95
00693864 Police, The – Best of	$19.95
00694975 Queen – Greatest Hits	$24.95
00690670 Queensryche – Very Best of	$19.95
00694910 Rage Against the Machine	$19.95
00690055 Red Hot Chili Peppers – Bloodsugarsexmagik	$19.95
00690584 Red Hot Chili Peppers – By the Way	$19.95
00690379 Red Hot Chili Peppers – Californication	$19.95
00690673 Red Hot Chili Peppers – Greatest Hits	$19.95

00690511 Reinhardt, Django – Definitive Collection	$19.95
00690643 Relient K – Two Lefts Don't Make a Right...But Three Do	$19.95
00690631 Rolling Stones – Guitar Anthology	$24.95
00690685 Roth, David Lee – Eat 'Em and Smile	$19.95
00690694 Roth, David Lee – Guitar Anthology	$24.95
00690749 Saliva – Survival of the Sickest	$19.95
00690031 Santana's Greatest Hits	$19.95
00690566 Scorpions – Best of	$19.95
00690659 Seger, Bob and the Silver Bullet Band – Greatest Hits, Volume 2	$17.95
00690604 Seger, Bob – Guitar Collection	$19.95
00690750 Shepherd, Kenny Wayne – The Place You're In	$19.95
00690419 Slipknot	$19.95
00690530 Slipknot – Iowa	$19.95
00690733 Slipknot – Vol. 3 (The Subliminal Verses)	$19.95
00120004 Steely Dan – Best of	$24.95
00694921 Steppenwolf – Best of	$22.95
00690689 Story of the Year – Page Avenue	$19.95
00690520 Styx Guitar Collection	$19.95
00120081 Sublime	$19.95
00690519 Sum 41 – All Killer No Filler	$19.95
00690612 Sum 41 – Does This Look Infected?	$19.95
00690606 System of a Down – Steal This Album	$19.95
00690531 System of a Down – Toxicity	$19.95
00694824 Taylor, James – Best of	$16.95
00694887 Thin Lizzy – Best of	$19.95
00690238 Third Eye Blind	$19.95
00690738 3 Doors Down – Away from the Sun	$22.95
00690737 3 Doors Down – The Better Life	$22.95
00690665 Thursday – War All the Time	$19.95
00690654 Train – Best of	$19.95
00690683 Trower, Robin – Bridge of Sighs	$19.95
00699191 U2 – Best of: 1980-1990	$19.95
00690732 U2 – Best of: 1990-2000	$19.95
00690039 Vai, Steve – Alien Love Secrets	$24.95
00690392 Vai, Steve – The Ultra Zone	$19.95
00690370 Vaughan, Stevie Ray and Double Trouble – The Real Deal: Greatest Hits Volume 2	$22.95
00690116 Vaughan, Stevie Ray – Guitar Collection	$24.95
00660058 Vaughan, Stevie Ray – Lightnin' Blues 1983-1987	$24.95
00694835 Vaughan, Stevie Ray – The Sky Is Crying	$22.95
00690015 Vaughan, Stevie Ray – Texas Flood	$19.95
00694789 Waters, Muddy – Deep Blues	$24.95
00690071 Weezer (The Blue Album)	$19.95
00690516 Weezer (The Green Album)	$19.95
00690447 Who, The – Best of	$24.95
00690596 Yardbirds, The – Best of	$19.95
00690696 Yeah Yeah Yeahs – Fever to Tell	$19.95
00690710 Yellowcard – Ocean Avenue	$19.95
00690443 Zappa, Frank – Hot Rats	$19.95
00690589 ZZ Top Guitar Anthology	$22.95